"The *Transformation Leader's Guide*. If anyone would have the accumulated wisdom to write a book with that title, it would be Bob Miles. This book ably and engagingly pulls from the arc of Miles's career, interweaving his academic interest in discovering basic principles of organizational change with his consulting engagements that put principles into practice. In a clear example of how theory and practice can inform and enrich each other, the book takes the reader through the complexity of large-scale change, with insights and examples that will be of use to scholars and those with transformational aspirations alike."
John R. Kimberly, *Bower Professor Emeritus, The Wharton School, University of Pennsylvania*

"Throughout his career, Bob Miles has been gifted in making sense of complex phenomena and organizing them into useful and understandable terms. In the chaotic and mystifying world of organizational transformation, Bob is among the very elite in capturing the essence of successful change. This book is a must read for leaders, change agents, scholars, and teachers who want to better understand how organizational transformation works, how to guide it, and how to help others implement it. This landmark book represents the summary of a lifetime of study and practice, and it is a rare treasure."
Kim S. Cameron, *Kelly Professor Emeritus of Management & Organizations, University of Michigan*

"This is an innovative and accomplished book by an author always at the centre of scholarship and practice in the field of leadership and change. Bob Miles articulates a grounded approach to corporate transformation built around the need to create, exploit and sustain positive energy for change over time. Crucial to the book's success is the step-by-step guide to top team leadership with its experience embedded in some of the great private and public sector organizations in the USA and beyond."
Andrew M. Pettigrew, *OBE, FBA, Emeritus Professor of Strategy and Organisation, Saïd Business School, University of Oxford*

"If you want advice about accomplishing successful organizational change Bob Miles is a great source. He has succeeded in accomplishing it and this book communicates his accumulated wisdom. It will facilitate your success!"
Jay W. Lorsch, *Kirstein Professor of Human Relations, Harvard Business School*

"Today's global business environment is full of turbulent seas. To navigate successfully you need to be able to steady your course with a solid strategy, adjust rapidly and keep everyone focused on their objectives. ACT is the seakeeping gyro that enables all of that and its creator, Bob Miles, has been the best corporate navigator in rough seas for decades. Over the last 27 years I have used the ACT Method for a variety of business voyages that required rapid transformation with wonderful results."
Rodger E. Smith, *Senior Vice President & General Manager, Oracle Utilities*

T0298631

TRANSFORMATION LEADER'S GUIDE

Sure to become the definitive guide for leaders facing the challenges of rapid enterprise-wide transformation, this book is the first detailed release of Robert H. Miles's proven Accelerated Corporate Transformation process – the ACT Method.

Many books on corporate transformation exist, often focusing on leadership styles and stories. This business manual goes further and deeper, providing frameworks, tools, and templates, to show what, when, and how a leader of enterprise-wide transformation should pace an organization through the essential transformation phases of Launch, Cascade, and Execute. The ACT approach is leader-led at all levels. It rapidly engages all employees and has reliably generated rapid breakthrough results across a wide variety of executive leaders, organizational types, and transformation challenges.

This Guide will be an indispensable resource for anyone leading or supporting a rapid transformation in their organization. Line managers, strategy consultants, learning and development professionals, human resources managers, and anyone interested in the inner workings of top leadership circles will appreciate the insights this book provides.

The Guide is also available as an online course, *Transformation Leader's Guide: The Online Course*.

Robert H. Miles, Ph.D., President of Corporate Transformation Resources (www.corptransform.com), has been the principal process architect of over thirty major corporate and institutional transformations, which have been documented in a series of books and a popular *Harvard Business Review* article on "Accelerating Corporate Transformations – Don't Lose Your Nerve!" Before launching his ACT practice, he served on the business school faculties at Alabama, Yale, Harvard, and Emory, and the Stanford Executive Institute.

TRANSFORMATION LEADER'S GUIDE

THE COMPLETE ACCELERATED CORPORATE TRANSFORMATION (ACT) METHOD

Robert H. Miles

Routledge
Taylor & Francis Group

NEW YORK AND LONDON

First published 2022
by Routledge
605 Third Avenue, New York, NY 10158

and by Routledge
4 Park Square, Milton Park, Abingdon, Oxon, OX14 4RN

Routledge is an imprint of the Taylor & Francis Group, an informa business

Library of Congress Cataloguing-in-Publication Data
Names: Miles, Robert H., author.
Title: Transformation leader's guide : the complete accelerated corporate transformation (ACT) method / Robert H. Miles.
Description: New York, NY : Routledge, 2022. | Includes bibliographical references and index. |
Identifiers: LCCN 2021056853 |
Subjects: LCSH: Organizational change. | Organizational learning. | Strategic planning. | Leadership.
Classification: LCC HD58.8 .M5264 2022 | DDC 658.4/06--dc23/eng/20220124
LC record available at https://lccn.loc.gov/2021056853

ISBN: 978-1-032-22481-7 (hbk)
ISBN: 978-1-032-22479-4 (pbk)
ISBN: 978-1-003-27272-4 (ebk)

DOI: 10.4324/9781003272724

Typeset in Palatino
by MPS Limited, Dehradun

Dedicated
to
Jane

CONTENTS

Robert H. Miles

ABOUT THE AUTHOR

Robert H. Miles, Ph.D., President, Corporate Transformation Resources, is a global thought and practice leader in the fields of corporate transformation and executive leadership. He has served CEOs as the principal process architect and supervisor of over 30 corporate transformations. A summary of insights from these experiences, titled *"Accelerating Corporate Transformations – Don't Lose Your Nerve!"* appeared as a feature article in the Jan/Feb 2010 issue of the Harvard Business Review. *Transformation Leader's Guide* (Routledge, 2022) is his career-spanning book on leading rapid, enterprise-wide transformation, which is complemented by his new online course, *Transformation Leader's Guide: The Online Course (2022).*

Over the past three decades, Bob has pioneered an *Accelerated Corporate Transformation (ACT)* methodology at such leading companies as Apple, Black & Veatch, General Electric, IBM Global Services, National Semiconductor, Office Depot, PGA Tour, Rockwell International, Southern Company and Symantec, as well as a number of emerging high-tech companies and public utilities. Miles also is the author of a series of books on corporate transformation including *Corporate Comeback* (Jossey-Bass/Wiley, 1997), *Leading Corporate Transformation* (Jossey-Bass/Wiley, 1997), and *BIG Ideas to BIG Results*, with Michael Kanazawa (2nd Edition, Pearson, 2016).

Frequently serving as a Process Architect to executive teams as they plan, launch, and execute their corporate transformation efforts, Bob helps new CEOS "take charge" and sitting CEOs launch the next major phase in their organization. A trademark of his approach has been the Rapid, High-engagement, All-employee Cascade™, which launches the execution phase by quickly focusing everyone in the enterprise on a shared set of performance and cultural initiatives targeted for breakthrough results.

On the Yale School of Management and Harvard Business School faculties for many years, Miles taught in the MBA, Doctoral, and executive programs. Bob was Chairman of an innovative executive residential program at Harvard, which helped CEOs and their teams plan corporate transformations. He is a co-founder of the Macro Organizational Behavior Society (Miles, **Macro Organizational Behavior**, 1980), a convocation of elected global scholars held each year at Harvard Business School; and he was elected Chairman of the Organization and Management Theory Division of the Academy of Management.

His other books include **The Organizational Life Cycle, Managing the Corporate Social Environment, The Regulatory Executives**, and **Coffin Nails and Corporate Strategies.**

Later, he was Isaac Stiles Hopkins Distinguished University Professor and Dean of the Faculty at the Goizueta Business School of Emory University.

Bob has served for over a decade as a faculty member at both the AEA/Stanford Executive Institute and at GE's Crotonville Operations. He also served on the Editorial Review Boards of Management Science and Administrative Science Quarterly, and on the Advisory Boards of the Organizational Effectiveness Division of The Conference Board and the U.S. Department of Energy.

Very early in his career, Bob was an Operations Analyst at Ford Motor Company, a First Lieutenant (Armor) in the U.S. Army, Special Assistant to the Director of Research, Development and Engineering at U.S. Army Missile Command, and a Project Manager at the Defense Advanced Research Projects Agency (DARPA) in the Office of the Secretary of Defense.

Miles received a B.S. from the McIntire School of Commerce at the University of Virginia (where he has served on the Advisory Board) and a Ph.D. in Business Administration from the University of North Carolina at Chapel Hill.

ACKNOWLEDGMENTS

I recently came across an article in one of the leading science journals which concluded that at least fifty percent of career success is due to luck. Thinking back, I couldn't agree more.

As I wind down work on my career-spanning book, I want to acknowledge the unexpected but indispensable support I have received from a special set of individuals at various times during my long professional career,

Heading the list are my early-career mentors.

Dr. John McDaniel, Director of the Research, Engineering and Development Laboratories of the U.S. Army Missile Command at Redstone Arsenal plucked me out of a cohort of junior officers assigned to him and appointed me his Special Assistant. John would prep me early Monday mornings on his agenda for the weekly staff meetings with the Lab Directors. Afterwards, he would have me debrief him on how I thought things went and what the next steps seemed appropriate. Before too long in this staff position, John promoted me as a project manager to the Defense Advanced Research Projects Agency (DARPA) in the Office of the U.S. Secretary of Defense. Yes, DARPA. Where the Internet was invented!

At DARPA I had the good fortune of being assigned a team of experts, headed by Professor Robert Thrall, Chair of the Department of Mathematical Sciences at the University of Michigan, along with two engineering professors, to help me manage a set of research projects. Before it came time for me to muster out of the Army, they convinced me to set aside plans to go to law school in favor of pursuing a Ph.D. When I asked them what field they recommended, they all agreed on "whatever interests you." Two months later I was enrolled in the doctoral program at the University of North Carolina in a brand new field called Organizational Behavior.

J. Stacy Adams, R J. Reynolds Professor of Applied Behavioral Science at the Kenan-Flagler School of Business at the University of North Carolina, an imminent global scholar who served as my Faculty Advisor, allowed me to break methodological ranks and pursue a self-designed, large-scale, field-based doctoral dissertation project. He not only modeled for me what it means to be a rigorous scholar but also what an abiding joy that pursuit would offer.

A few years later, when I joined the faculty of the new Yale School of Management, what we needed most were current case studies for our new Master's curriculum. Having read a local newspaper about a big transition from being product-focused to becoming market-focused that was being pursued by a Hartford-based insurance company, I naively called Aetna before normal working hours to obtain permission to write a case on the blurb. To my great luck, Bill Bailey, the President of Aetna, picked up the phone and listened patiently before informing me that the company in the paper was "Little Aetna," whereas his was "Big Aetna!" And with only a moment's pause, he related that this was a pretty good idea, and asked if I would be able to join a team reporting to him to guide a similar transformation of Big Aetna. This is how I came upon the opportunity to become immersed in my first multi-year corporate transformation project.

Then jumping a half-decade ahead, when I ended up on the Harvard Business School faculty, I began work with a new colleague, Professor Michael Beer, a rare "practice-focused scholar," who soon thereafter chose me to succeed him as Faculty Chair of his innovative program for CEOs and members of their teams. This good fortune enabled me to intimately observe on the Harvard campus multiple executive teams at a time grapple with planning corporate and public transformations.

Next came Noel Tichy, a full Professor at Michigan and leading global expert in his own right in transformational leadership who, while serving as the head of GE's Crotonville (executive education and development) Operation, invited me to join a small elite consulting team charged with supporting new CEO Jack Welch's initial wave of transformation of General Electric. This endeavor, which spanned several years, sensitized me to the importance of speed, simplicity and action learning in large-scale, enterprise-wide transformation; constructs that would play equally well with many high-tech leaders in Silicon Valley.

Sometime later in midst of my corporate transformation practice, there were three Transformation Leaders each of whom I served as principal process architect on multiple rapid, enterprise-wide transformation projects. These serial engagements with different Transformation Leaders provided an unusually rich source for refining my understanding about how to accelerate corporate transformations.

I worked closely with Dr. Gilbert F. Amelio on integrating multiple internal divisions and external acquisitions into the top-performing business unit in Rockwell International's portfolio; again, on the dramatic turnaround of National Semiconductor, the famous "Animals of Silicon Valley;" and finally, to staunch the hemorrhaging of Apple Computer and pave the way for Steve Job's return to the company.

Then there were another three successive transformation projects, first involving Southern Company, at the time Fortune's "Most Admired" U.S. electric utility making over a billion dollars in profits a year. Their enterprise-wide transformation project converted ninety-two fossil and hydro plants across five States, each with its own employee union, into a Generation Company. Next followed PricewaterhouseCoopers, where my Accelerated Corporate Transformation (ACT) methodology was used to launch two new businesses, and then, Black & Veatch, where the ACT Method was deployed to dramatically improve profitability and leaven the traditional engineering culture, all under the leadership of Rodger Smith, who now heads Oracle's global utility business.

Third, there was a series of dramatic, high-tech, ACT-based transformations led by Dr. Bami Bastani, who now heads the Mobile and Wireless Business of Global Foundries.

Next, there is Donis Leach, who for over a quarter-century has served as my research assistant in support of both my ACT-based transformation projects and the books I have written about them. All during those years, we have lived in opposite corners of the United States. Nevertheless, I cannot imagine launching any of these projects without her intelligence, diligence, and good humor.

I also want to express my appreciation to Michael Kanazawa, who I first met when he joined the transformation Process Support Team of Pacific Telesis Group, a major West Coast telecom client where he was Director of Corporate Strategy. He has been a close collaborator on many corporate transformation projects and co-author of two books on the ACT Method. With that experience, he went on to build and sell an innovation firm to Ernst & Young, where he currently serves as a Principal in the practice areas of innovation and transformation.

Then there was the very good luck of securing a stellar publishing house for this book in midst of the Covid pandemic chaos in the publishing industry. I cannot thank enough the following members of the Routledge editorial and production staff for their flexibility and smooth delivery of the *Transformation Leader's Guide*. Among the key players were Meredith Norwood, Chloe Herbert, and Sumit Kumar.

Most important was my very good luck of moving to a high school in a different town and at just the right time where I met Jane, my wife and life partner, who's sacrifice and support has been enduring and sustaining. A professional in psychology, public policy and volunteerism in her own right, Jane has also held our family and social life together while making notable contributions to the communities in which we have lived and enabling me to stay the course that culminated in the development of the ACT Method for leading rapid, enterprise-wide transformations.

PREFACE

Ask any leader who has overseen an organizational transformation what should have been handled differently, and you are likely to get this answer: "I should have—and could have—moved faster."

Such executives have a long list of regrets: They wish they had unified the leadership team right away. They wish they had engaged employees sooner and quickly drummed up support for the new vision. They wish they hadn't waited so long to test their assumptions and refine their key initiatives. And they wish they had generated some visible returns early on, to accelerate the commitments and reinforce the expectations of employees, customers, suppliers, and investors.[1]

Any transformation—launching the next major phase in an organization, pivoting to a new strategy to achieve breakthrough performance, enabling a new executive leader to take charge, or integrating an acquisition—is fraught with challenges. Several decades ago, I began chairing an innovative program that convened groups of CEOs and members of their executive team for two-week, in-residence sessions at Harvard Business School. They applied to the program by sending us a written summary of the major challenge confronting their organization. We admitted teams that reported having the biggest challenges, which we came to refer to as transformation challenges.

During their time on campus, they collaborated with faculty members and peers from noncompeting companies on solving their most serious challenge, and they left with rudimentary plans to be fleshed out and implemented when they returned to work. They reconvened nine months later, in a short program on the Harvard campus that we called "Learning from Changing," to share their experiences and sharpen their "re-plan" before returning to the scenes of their transformation.[2]

Within a few years, a clear pattern emerged from the program: The biggest barrier to transformation success was getting organizations to execute their bold new ideas quickly before energy and enthusiasm dissipated and new and traditional competitors roared by. Armed with those early insights, I left the Harvard faculty to become directly involved in more than 30 enterprise-wide transformations. Most put me at the right hand of new or sitting CEOs, as principal process architect, for periods ranging from two to three years. That I was able to support 2, sometimes 3 corporate transformations simultaneously, attests to the efficacy of the leader-led, not consultant-led, process architecture I deployed and refined over the years.

Not long ago, I participated in a series of meetings with a couple of Harvard Business Review editors for the purpose of distilling *why* this approach to transformation, which came to be called Accelerated Corporate Transformation, or ACT, had been so successful across a wide variety of organization types and transformation challenges. The result was an article, *"Accelerating Corporate Transformations – Don't Lose Your Nerve!"* which identified the key elements of ACT that enabled these transformation leaders to quickly deliver on their big promises.

Although most ACT-guided transformations have taken place in the private sector, a large minority of them have also been highly successful in other sectors. Indeed, going all the way back to the Harvard program, a few alternative sector organizations were usually in the mix with corporate teams in each session. Over the years since then, ACT has been successfully deployed in a variety of business enterprises in the United States and abroad, including several of the iconic corporate transformations of our time. But it has also successfully guided the transformation of many other types of organizations, including government agencies, public utilities, hospitals, whole healthcare systems, and even the PGA Tour. So, I think it is fair to say that with a bit of tinkering around the edges, the implementation-focused ACT game plan is generic.

TRANSFORMATION INSIGHTS

Based primarily on all this direct experience, plus paying attention to transformations attempts in my peripheral vision, it became obvious that many talented executives don't fully appreciate the following subtle but powerful insights into leading a transformation:

- Transformation launches must be *bold* and *rapid* to succeed.
- Yet, embedded in most organizations are six *"inhibitors"* that can slow things down to a grinding pace.
- During business-as-usual periods, these embedded inhibitors may be irritating, but their effects on performance are reasonably benign.
- However, during a transformation, which requires bold, rapid action, *any one* of the inhibitors can derail the larger effort.
- To have the best chance of accelerating their transformations, leaders need to identify, engage, and overcome each of these embedded inhibitors in a *particular sequence*.

The remainder of the book illustrates how and when to engage and overcome each of the inhibitors using the Accelerated Corporate Transformation (ACT) methodology, for which corresponding *"accelerators"* serve as cornerstones.

Meaning of Transformation

But first, let's explore the meaning of Transformation that is the focus here, and identify the types of transformational challenges executive leaders typically face. In the context of executive leadership, transformation may be broadly conceived as "a few well-articulated initiatives targeted for breakthrough results in a short period of time ... in a sea of necessary incremental improvements." In my first book on transformation, *Leading Corporate Transformation*, the challenge posed to would-be transformation leaders in the opening sentence read, "How can I achieve fundamental transformation without exposing my organization to unacceptable risk?"[3]

Just how big is the task of planning, launching, and leading an organization-wide, top-to-bottom transformation? A premier global management consulting firm recently reported in an in-house article titled *"How to Beat the Transformation Odds,"* that over 73% of business transformations fail! Terrible news for employees, customers, and societies. Is there little wonder why the vast majority of transformation leaders miss the mark by a wide margin?[4]

EXHIBIT 0.1   Transformation[5]

In a similar vein, a leading outplacement and executive coaching firm recently reported that the average CEO tenure of the largest corporations dropped from 8.5 years in 2003 to 3.7 years by 2020. Similarly, in 2019 the Asia-Pacific market saw one of its highest turnover rates in the past decade.[6] Both sharp trends reinforce the need for competency in transformation leadership, with a specific emphasis on speed of execution.

As you get into this book, you will find the *accelerators* useful levers to ramp up to speed with your effort without overburdening managers and employees. You will see how to run a crisp, streamlined transformation launch process in parallel with the day-to-day management process, and be able to eventually meld the two. You will come to value some upfront investments in people and process that will actually speed your effort to early alignment and engagement and ultimately, breakthrough results. But the book will certainly fail its purpose if you put it down not understanding that speed through simplicity and compression trumps the otherwise enormous complexity that overwhelms many transformation leaders.

Transformation and Complexity

It has taken quite a journey to distill the essence out of the full complexity of reliably leading a successful transformation. Along the way, I came across a saying that pretty much sums up that journey. It was one of Chief Justice

Oliver Wendell Holmes' gems: *"I wouldn't give a fig for the simplicity on this side of complexity, but I would give my life for the simplicity on the other side of complexity."* Thankfully, after all the years of practice and reflection, the ACT Method resides on the "other" side of the full complexity of transformation. The same is not true for most transformation leaders.

Many new transformation leaders find themselves in the captain's chair for the first time in their career – on the wrong side of complexity. For sure, they would not have been chosen for such consequential responsibility – sometimes involving the future of hundreds of thousands of employees – had they not logged many career successes and mastered many essential skills. But there is no transformation-level practice field, where rising executives can fully prepare for the big leadership job.

To illustrate this point, I recall being up on the flybridge heading out to sea from Chatham at the elbow of Cape Cod. It was a perfect day – clear, no wind, ideal temperature and when we rounded the Coast Guard station there were no red flags – until it wasn't. No sooner had we entered the narrow channel, with family aboard aft, granddaughter beside me on the tower and son on the bow looking for sand bars than I spied about 100 yards out the making of a *very* tall, rogue wave.

In my 40 years at sea, 30 of them right off where we were, I had never encountered firsthand such a beast. I could cut and run, risking a broach that might land everyone overboard. Or I could drop the hammers, charge up the wave's wall and hope the tonnage of the vessel would punch us through.

In a blink, I ordered everyone below to grab a seat, my son off the bow, and my granddaughter to hold tight on the fish tower as I slammed the twin engines to full speed ahead. A moment later the wave struck, and after a few agonizing seconds, we almost went vertical before punching through. The drop to the other side was jarring, but thankfully, no one was hurt, and we were safe.

What prepared me to rise to that once-in-a-lifetime occasion? Nothing in my previous experience, for sure. However, a couple of years before, I had the good luck to see how a sea captain attempted to deal with an even bigger rogue in the movie, *The Perfect Storm*!

If you're new to the transformation leader role, it's very helpful to have luck, but don't plan on it.

Shape of Transformation Failure

At the other extreme, far too many transformation attempts begin with an enormous amount of preparation work and fanfare before assuming a shape not too different from the one shown below. Often the up-front analytical work dwarfs, in both money and time spent, the launch and execution effort. Attention and focus are never really captured before launch, so new transformation initiatives soon erode from the "this too will pass" syndrome. Before long, the leader sees this as a lost cause, at which time a new transformation czar is tapped down below; and the outcomes curve continues to approach zero as a limit until someone announces the coming of the next new thing!

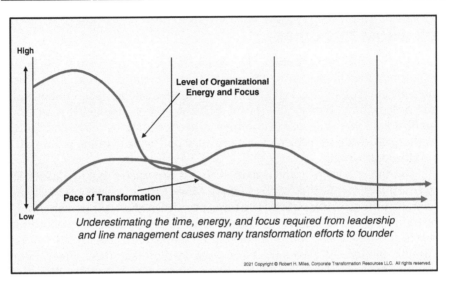

EXHIBIT 0.2   Typical Stages of a Failed Transformation Effort

High

Level of Organizational
Energy and Focus

Pace of Transformation

Low

*Underestimating the time, energy, and focus required from leadership
and line management causes many transformation efforts to founder*

VISION FOR THIS GUIDE

The *Transformation Leader's Guide* is intended to become the definitive guide for executive leaders in this domain. It represents the distillation of over 30 rapid, CEO-led corporate transformations for which I served as principal process architect and supervisor.

The *Guide* will enable an executive leader, the extended leadership team, and the support staff to reliably plan, launch, and orchestrate a rapid, enterprise-wide transformation as well as enlist, equip, and empower the manager and employee populations to lead the effort at their levels.

The *Guide* outlines in detail the proven **Accelerated Corporate Transformation (ACT)** methodology, with supporting frameworks, tools, and templates. It lays out with rich examples of many iconic ACT-based corporate transformations what, when and how a leader of enterprise-wide transformation should pace an organization through the essential Focus, Align, Cascade, and Execute Phases. One that is leader-led at all levels, that rapidly engages all employees, and that has proven to reliably generate rapid breakthrough results across a wide variety of executive leaders, organizational types, and transformation challenges.

The *Guide* will also reveal a number of powerful new constructs that must be understood and carefully orchestrated by the Transformation Leader and support team.

The novel approach identifies embedded *"inhibitors"* in all organizations that although mildly irritating under normal – steady-state, incremental-improvement – conditions, any one of which can easily derail the launch and execution of a transformation. The *Guide* also reveals corresponding *"accelerators"* that leaders must deploy to engage and overcome each inhibitor to ensure rapid transformation success, and it integrates them into the roadmap of the ACT Method.

FOR WHOM THIS GUIDE?

For whom is this book written? The quick answer is the mighty CEOs and their senior leadership teams through whom dramatic, iconic institutional transformations flow. You will learn about them and their roles in engaging and overcoming the inhibitors to transformation embedded in their organization. You will learn how they can effectively develop and launch an enterprise-wide transformation game plan and rapidly guide it through to breakthrough results.

But the species of transformation that is articulated here is leader-led, not consultant- or staff-led. A rare breed. Moreover, it is *leader-led at all levels* of a transforming organization. The same principles and tools that are used at the senior executive level are streamlined for deployment by subordinate leaders and managers, and ultimately to all employees. The cascade process is double looped. At each successive level, leaders take their direct reports through the same launch and execution steps and processes they went through with their boss, and so on down the chain in a double-loop fashion.

Along the journey, everyone learns from doing a variety of valuable leadership skills, including how to structure a major improvement effort and what processes may be deployed to speed it to success. How to use speed to advantage, by simplifying plans and compressing processes. How to create "safe passage" to support dialogue and critical decision making. How to sharpen a transformation initiative and simplify it before implementation. How to really engage people at all levels. Things like that and many more.

Which is to say, by using the transformation game plan outlined herein, it is entirely possible to rapidly achieve breakthrough results while improving manager and people skills and elevating the culture and agility of your organization. In this sense, execution of the transformation game plan revealed in this book generates substantial side-benefits in terms of management and organization development.

To be more specific about the audiences most likely to benefit from the *Guide*, the most relevant would be as follows:

Those Responsible

The *Guide* should become indispensable to those responsible for orchestrating a "live" rapid transformation in their organization. This would include not only the Transformation Leader, but certainly the next several levels of management below. Also, within a transforming enterprise, human resource professionals represent the most likely discipline to be asked to prescribe and support a transformation game plan. More often than not, they are the first responders to the Transformation Leader's call to action. Then leaders at all levels could benefit from such a guidebook. And the cascading process to all employees could best be comprehended within the context provided by the book.

Those Intensely Interested in Leadership

The *Guide* should also be attractive to the vast multitude of people with an interest in "Leadership" writ large. The book would provide this vast cohort access to how things really work at the top of the "leadership pyramid" to successfully rise to an institution transformation challenge.

Those in Professional Practice

Advising on corporate transformations is the life blood of many global management consultancies. Proprietary approaches to transformation are the crown jewels of such professional service firms. The surprise availability of ACT on a silver platter may be attractive to consultants and consultancies, especially in the fields of leadership, strategy, general and functional management, organization development, organizational behavior, executive coaching, and human resource management. And the core ACT Roadmap may serve as the backbone from which complementary methodologies may be affixed (e.g., tactical change management and incremental improvement routines, design-centered approaches, social media tools, and agile business principles).

Those in Management Development Centers and Corporate Universities

There are places of learning where the *Guide* could be of special relevance. Executive development programs, corporate universities, modules in upper-level classes in undergraduate- and graduate-level courses in leadership and management come to mind.

STRUCTURE OF THE GUIDE

The structure of the book is straightforward. It follows the all-important *Roadmap* upon which the ACT-based transformation game plan is draped.

The first two chapters are essential for the internal diagnosis of the reality confronting the organization. Fresh new ground for the ACT Method. Chapter One introduces the major *inhibitors* of rapid transformation, and it provides a brief *Readiness Survey* the reader may take to better understand the inhibitors embedded in his or her organization. Your results will quickly reveal the intensity of resistance the inhibitors pose should a transformation challenge arise. Chapter Two identifies the antidotes to the inhibitors, called *accelerators*, which underpin the ACT Method.

The middle chapters integrate new insights and refinements that have been grafted onto the ACT fundamentals and show how Transformation Leaders should go about launching and driving the ACT Accelerators.

Chapter Three introduces the Accelerated Corporate Transformation *game plan*, and Chapters Four and Five discuss the architecture of the ACT-based plan in terms of its essential *structure*s and processes.

The next chapters walk you through the major phases of the *Roadmap* – the backbone of a rapid transformation. They include the *Focus, Align, Engage* and *Execute Phases*, and cover not only the core concepts but also provide you with the tools, templates, and case studies from the ACT practice to get your transformation job done.

Chapter 10 provides a comprehensive summary of what it takes to be an effective leader of transformation, wherever you reside in an organization.

COMPLEMENTARY ONLINE COURSE

Finally, the *Guide* has been distilled into an online course, called *Transformation Leader's Guide: The Online Course*. Organized along with the ACT transformation Phases from Confronting Reality through the Replanning for Year Two, the video-based course consists of 10 Learning Modules including 47 Lessons. For more information about the course, please reach me by email (rmiles@corptransform.com) or access my website (www.corptransform.com); or order directly from Flevy at (https://flevy.com/program/act). This self-paced course could be helpful in enabling you to distill the major takeaways from the ACT Method described in detail in this book. It may help speed the orientation of those who are initially on point or remote during your transformation launch.

For example, supervisors and employees at all levels may access the online course on a just-in-time basis as they prepare for each phase of the ACT-based transformation roadmap. Also, the video-based course can take learners to the front lines of other actual transformation launches, making many of the ACT constructs and frameworks more vivid and understandable.

Welcome to the exciting and fulfilling world of accelerated corporate transformation. It has been my privilege to work at this frontier for almost my entire career. It is my hope that you will find indispensable insights in this Guide to help you successfully rise to the big challenges that loom ahead in your leadership career.

Notes

1. Many of the insights discussed in this Preface and in Chapters 1 and 2 are expanded from Robert H. Miles, *"Accelerating Corporate Transformations – Don't Lose Your Nerve!"* Harvard Business Review, January-February 2010.

2. I am grateful to Michael Beer, the Cahners-Rabb Professor, Emeritus, at Harvard Business School, who founded and led this innovative Harvard program and later passed the Faculty Chair reigns to me. Beer, my first encounter with a "practice-focused scholar," became a career-redefining role model.

3. Robert H. Miles, Leading Corporate Transformation: A Blueprint for Business Renewal. San Francisco: Josey-Bass Publishers, A Division of John Wiley & Sons, 1997, p. 1.

4. David Jacquemont, David Maor and Angelika Reich, *"How to Beat the Transformation Odds,"* McKinsey Quarterly, April 2015.

5. Stock photo from Shutterstock.com

6. Lisa Smyth, Report on Challenger, Gray and Christmas Report, "Adapt or Die: Why being a CEO is More Challenging Than Ever," CEO Magazine, July 22, 2020.

CHAPTER 1

Transformation Leader's Challenge

Gauging Readiness for Rapid Corporate Transformation

The Embedded "Inhibitors" to Rapid Transformation

No transformation challenge is greater than the one confronting you when you assume the mantel of executive leadership. Yet most executives only get a chance or two at most in their long careers to get this right.

From the moment their appointment is announced, new executives must quickly develop their plans for "taking charge" and for launching the next major phase in their organization. The transformation game plan they need to develop with their colleagues not only requires a re-examination of the organization's external and internal realities, strategies, and guiding purpose but also quite often a re-shaping of its management process and culture, a fundamental re-alignment of its organization, and a re-engagement of its managers and employees. A reboot of the total system.

GAUGING TRANSFORMATION "READINESS"

When rising to such a career- and institution-defining challenge, it is critical for you to be able to accurately gauge your organization's *readiness* to move forward boldly and rapidly before developing your transformation game plan. This starting point begins with recognition of the existence of embedded "inhibitors" in your organization, which although benign in their effects during steady-state conditions become major impediments to transformative change. Indeed, when it comes time for you to "take charge," any one of these inhibitors can derail the whole effort if left unattended.[1]

Let's start by identifying the embedded inhibitors to rapid transformation in *all* organizations. At the end of this chapter, you will be given an

DOI: 10.4324/9781003272724-1

opportunity to gauge their intensity in *your* organization. And in the chapters that follow, we will articulate a proven Accelerated Corporate Transformation (ACT) methodology that was explicitly designed to enable a leader to engage and overcome each inhibitor to rapid transformation success.

THE TRANSFORMATION "INHIBITORS"

Six embedded inhibitors will likely be encountered in any rapid transformation attempt. Five may be expected to emerge during your planning and launch stages and the sixth will appear at predictable waypoints during your first year of execution. Each will need to be anticipated, engaged, and overcome. This is a major role that you and your supporting cast will need to play very well.

Inhibitor #1: Cautious Management Culture

Executives keep their heads down, protect their business and try to avoid big mistakes by sticking to the tried and true.

When the call for transformation first goes out, managers and employees are usually immersed in activities that reinforce the existing business model. People are engaged in a deep routine of doing their own thing, supporting their own slice of the organization, and getting rewarded for it. There initially is no incentive to speak out with big, bold ideas to support the new transformation challenge. Contributing to this initial pattern of avoidance is fear about the unknown, the unproven, and the incomplete.

Managers and employees will have arrived at this moment of transformation launch by successfully mastering the competencies required by the business model being replaced. Finally, most employees will have seen managerial initiatives and mandates come and go; so, there will tend to exist at the moment of transformation launch, a vein of uncertainty that runs throughout the organization about the leader's commitment to stay the course. All these elements contribute to cautiousness in the management culture about signing on to the leader's new transformation agenda.

Inhibitor #2: Business-as-Usual Management Process

Day-to-day management processes are already overtaxed and there's no room for anything new or different.

Any attempt to plan and launch the next phase in an organization by relying on the existing day-to-day management process will initially receive short shrift because the agendas of all those routinely scheduled meetings will already be overcrowded. Indeed, you will always find executives waiting in the hallways, just hoping to get in for five minutes to present their ideas. The Business-as-Usual Management Process is also typically preoccupied with incremental improvements and quarterly plans and reviews, not new directions or breakthrough results. Attention to a new transformation agenda or initiative will be deferred until someone has come up with the "perfect" new model. Finally, within the existing business-as-usual process, only a few executives will be intimately involved with the CEO in planning the transformation and in defining its major initiatives. Hence, when it comes time to implement, the rest of the senior executives who have been in the dark will cast large shadows over their parts of the enterprise, leading to misunderstanding and misalignment down below during execution.

Inhibitor #3: Initiative Gridlock

> *Too many separate initiatives are being thrown at the organization and its people at the same time.*

In most organizations, over time you can witness the accretion of layer upon layer of incremental improvement initiatives. Sometimes this happens because of the proliferation of well-intended, but uncoordinated functional initiatives, in which each department team, with the best of intentions, attempts to drive improvements from their functional perspective throughout the enterprise. In other instances, initiative gridlock emerges because the new leader lacks the courage to focus his or her organization on a few important initiatives to achieve early returns, learn from mistakes, shed outmoded projects, and redouble the effort behind the initiatives chosen to achieve breakthrough results. The consequence is task overload throughout the organization. This is the typical environment into which a leader's new transformation challenge dumps yet another set of initiatives on top of many existing ones, creating widespread gridlock.

Inhibitor #4: Recalcitrant Executives

> *Some executives remain unconvinced and uncommitted regarding the new leader's transformation agenda.*

Protracted tolerance of nonaligned, uncommitted, or incapable leaders can most certainly derail any corporate transformation attempt. This is particularly the case for very senior executives who hold sway over large parts of the enterprise and whose skills at their advanced career stage may be out of sync with those required by the leader's new transformation agenda. Many of these key executives will be loath to alter the regimes they are already pursuing in the part of the organization for which they are responsible. They may resist requests by the Transformational Leader to re-allocate resources to help unproven or underperforming units develop, newer departments that may be better aligned with the transformation agenda. Finally, conflict avoidance on the part of some CEOs may cause them to allow recalcitrant executives to persist in their traditional ways and thereby undermine the organization's transformation progress.

Involving *all* members of the senior leadership team in tackling the first three to four inhibitors can help many initially reluctant executives find a way to not only come aboard but also actively champion the new transformation agenda. So, don't try to take on Inhibitor #4 fully before you've worked with your senior team on identifying, engaging, and overcoming the first three inhibitors. Remember, the *sequence* by which you engage and overcome each inhibitor is important for transformation success.

Inhibitor #5: Disengaged Employees

Employees are always one big step behind leaders, putting the organization out of alignment and leaving employees disengaged.

Employee disengagement is a primary reason for corporate transformation failures; so, it is important for a transformational leader to address this inhibitor before moving forward into execution. What do you see when you encounter disengaged people? Disengaged managers and employees often do not understand the need for transformation. They do not grasp the new strategy and transformation agenda. They may work hard, but do not know where to best focus their efforts. They don't believe they will be rewarded for their mastery of new behaviors and skills required by the transformation. Many will have experienced failed transformations and will assume "this too will pass." Finally, disengaged employees will not know how to lead the transformation at their level in the organization.

Inhibitor #6: Loss of Focus During Execution

Just when the transformation effort seems to be taking hold, execution hits another slump in momentum.

By the time your transformation process shifts into the Execute Phase, some of your executive leaders may have become lulled into a state of exhaustion. They may wish to think that all that positive energy and intense focus achieved during the Planning and Launch phases will automatically be transferred and sustained during the Execute Phase. Falsely reassured, such leaders all too quickly delegate the transformation oversight and follow through to others before moving on to "shiny" new challenges. Such leadership behaviors are in direct contrast to what is actually required during the first year of execution.

During the first full performance year under a new transformation game plan, you can expect to encounter no less than three predictable "slumps" in energy and focus during the Execute Phase, which if unanticipated and unheeded can derail the transformation effort – just as surely as any of the five inhibitors encountered during the Planning and Launch phases.

The first predictable slump is the "Post-launch Blues," which involves a desire on the part of leaders to relax immediately following a bold launch. After several months of distraction from their involvement in transformation planning, some executives reach their limit in being able to juggle their responsibilities for planning and launching the transformation while running their part of the day-to-day business. So, you are likely to hear something soon after launch like, "Hey, we're over the hump!" For many, this will signal their return to business as usual, which everyone in their part of the organization will surely notice and imitate.

The second predictable slump, "Mid-course Overconfidence," will emerge about halfway or two-thirds of the way through the first performance execution year. By that time, the transformation vessel will have cleared the harbor, many important things will appear to be on course, and the tendency will be to set the sails, lash down the tiller, and sit back to enjoy the smooth sailing. This kind of early complacency can sap important energy, learning, and focus that are so critical to keeping the transformation momentum on pace and on course.

The final predictable slump comes near the end of the first performance year. Called the "Presumption of Perpetual Motion," this slump is based on the belief that by year end things are progressing so well that there is no need to re-examine, re-plan, and re-launch the effort at the beginning of the next performance year. Of course, nothing could be more ill-advised.

THE "READINESS" SURVEY

To enable you to conduct a quick assessment of what you are going to be up against as you take charge to develop and lead your transformation game plan, take a moment to complete the simple diagnostic survey given in Exhibit 1.1.

You may wonder if the six inhibitors are more-or-less troublesome for transformation attempts in organizations, industries, or sectors different than your own. Summarized in the bar chart in Exhibit 1.2 is the intensity of inhibitor ratings of the top three levels of executives at the transformation launch of their large organizations under my supervision across a variety of industries, sectors, and transformation game plans. The very high-intensity scores across all these transformation settings reinforce the assertion that the six inhibitors are ubiquitous, and that dealing with *all* of them is a requirement for rapid transformation success.

Knowing the magnitude of these inhibitors in your organization is the first step in engaging and overcoming them. Developing a corporate transformation game plan that takes each of them into account will make all the difference in your success during these fast-paced, disruptive times.

This perspective prescribes a skill set that all executive leaders, managers, and human resource professionals must master to lead rapid transformations. Moreover, awareness of these inhibitors and how to overcome them (later in the book) will empower and engage supervisors and employees throughout the organization and enable them to better lead the transformation in their areas of responsibility.

TIPS FOR ASSESSING READINESS/THE INHIBITORS

- Make your first step in the *Prework* leading up to the launch of your transformation an assessment of your organization's readiness for transformation.
- Have each member of the top three levels of leadership to complete the *Readiness Assessment Survey* and share its results with them as part of your initial *Confronting Reality* event. (To assure individual confidentiality, report only the average rating of each inhibitor by level.)
- Understand the intensity of each embedded *inhibitor* in your organization, and make sure your transformation game plan covers how you and your leadership team are going to engage and overcome each one of them.

EXHIBIT 1.1   "Readiness" Survey

The Six Inhibitors

Inhibitor	Description	Irrelevant	Not Very Important	Somewhat Important	Important	Critical
Cautious Management Culture	• Deep routine of doing one's own thing and getting rewarded for it • Often working very hard on existing business model • Fear of the unknown, unproven and incomplete • Uncertainty about leader's commitment to stay the course • Little incentive to speak out with big, bold, new ideas	1	2	3	4	5
Business-as-Usual Management Process	• Attempts to plan and launch the next phase within the day-to-day management process, whose agenda is already overcrowded • Only a few executives involved in defining the major transformation initiatives • Preoccupation with incremental improvements; not breakthrough results • Waiting for the perfect new business model	1	2	3	4	5
Initiative Gridlock	• Lack of courage on the part of leaders to focus their organization • Layering one initiative on top of another • Uncoordinated functional initiatives • Not staying with an initiative long enough to achieve early results and learn • Feeling of task overload in the organization	1	2	3	4	5
Recalcitrant Executives	• Protracted tolerance of nonaligned, uncommitted or incapable executives • Conflict avoidance by the executive leader • Reluctance of executives to re-allocate their resources to support the transformation agenda • Anxiety about personal competencies needed to perform	1	2	3	4	5
Disengaged Employees	• Employees do not understand the need for transformation • They do not grasp the new strategy and transformation agenda • They may work hard, but are not sure where to focus their efforts • They don't feel safe in sharing their best ideas • They are not certain they will be rewarded for the new expected behaviors • They do not know how to lead the transformation at their level in the organization	1	2	3	4	5
Loss of Focus During Execution	• Desire to relax immediately following launch of new initiatives • Tendency to put everything on auto-pilot once things appear to be on track • Belief that things are progressing well, with no need to re-plan and re-launch at the beginning of the next performance year	1	2	3	4	5

How important will it be to deal with this Inhibitor in launching the transformation of my firm?

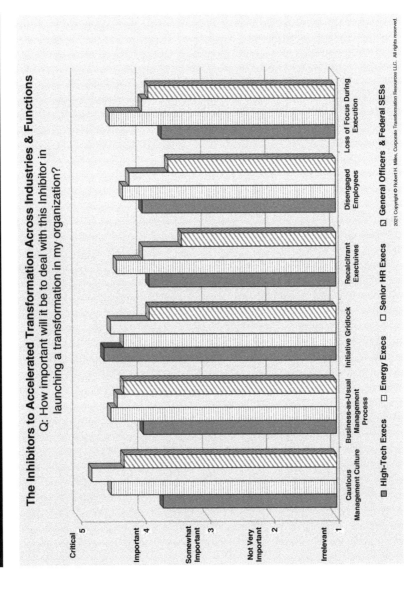

EXHIBIT 1.2   The Inhibitor Ratings Across Sectors

The Inhibitors to Accelerated Transformation Across Industries & Functions
Q: How important will it be to deal with this Inhibitor in launching a transformation in my organization?

Note

1. The discovery and articulation of the six embedded inhibitors to rapid, organization-wide transformation were first revealed in Robert H. Miles, "Accelerating Corporate Transformations: Don't Lose Your Nerve!" Harvard Business Review, January–February 2010. This chapter expands on the meaning of the embedded inhibitors and the role they play in transformation leadership. Reprinted with permission from Harvard Business Press. Copyright 2010 by Harvard Business Publishing; all rights reserved.

CHAPTER 2

The Transformation Leader's Accelerators

"Preparation is important, but not at the expense of motion."

Experience over the past three decades as process architect and orchestrator of dozens of accelerated organizational transformations across a wide variety of industries and business challenges not only revealed the primary Inhibitors that cause leadership failure but also enabled me to discover and verify the most powerful corresponding *Accelerators* to overcome them.[1]

Accelerators enable a leader to engage and overcome the transformation Inhibitors. The pairings shown in the exhibit below have held up regardless of variations in leaders, settings, and transformation challenges. Ranging from the turnaround of National Semiconductor, the "Animals of Silicon Valley" who became "Silicon Valley's Comeback Company of the Year,"[2] to the launch of the growth phase at the newly formed IBM Global Services and the total system realignment of a series of big-box retailers and regional electrical utilities, to the succession process of an outside minister from the West Coast to one of the largest churches in the Southeast and the merger and integration of major community and university healthcare systems, as well as the "taking charge" process at the PGA Tour, when an inside attorney succeeded the Commissioner who was a golfing legend (Exhibit 2.1).

Across all this diversity confronting new and sitting Transformation Leaders, the pivotal roles played by the Inhibitors and Accelerators became firmer and clearer. They gradually became the essential elements of a methodology I refer to as "Accelerated Corporate Transformation," or simply ACT, which we will take up in depth during the second part of the book.

But for now, let's focus in this chapter on each of the Accelerators and how they enable a leader to overcome the Inhibitors and achieve organizational transformation in record time. We will begin with the Accelerator that best equips a Transformation Leader to engage and overcome the first Inhibitor, "Cautious Management Culture."

DOI: 10.4324/9781003272724-2

EXHIBIT 2.1   Transformation Accelerators

Embedded Inhibitors	Transformation Accelerators
1 Cautious Management Culture	1 Mandatory Participation with "Safe Passage"
2 "Business-as-Usual" Management Process	2 The "No-Slack" Launch
3 Initiative Gridlock	3 Deliberately Compressed Agenda
4 Recalcitrant Executives	4 Committed & Capable Change Leaders
5 Disengaged Employees	5 Top-to-Bottom Employee Buy-In
6 Loss of Focus During Execution	6 Anticipation of Execution "Slumps"

ACCELERATOR #1: MANDATORY PARTICIPATION WITH "SAFE PASSAGE"

When organizations pursue variations on the same success model for an extended period, they become preoccupied with incremental improvement. Rather than teeing up big ideas and targeting big results, executive decision-makers try to avoid big mistakes. They hunker down in their respective areas of responsibility, believing they are too busy with daily operations to get involved in reimagining the entire business. The problem is that transforming an enterprise requires intensive cooperation among executive peers. Strong traditional units must share resources with unproven or underperforming units, and often they must sacrifice something they value for the good of the whole.

An incremental, parochial mindset also affirms the traditional executive pecking order. Those who control the most resources or institutional assets tend to monopolize discussions, trump new ideas, and strong-arm decision-making, thereby reinforcing the status quo. The management culture in the U.S. automotive industry was so cautious a few decades back that some of the "big car" majors decided to create geographically separate greenfield subsidiaries, to free up the executive attention and the design and development resources needed to respond to the small-car challenge of foreign competitors.

In a conservative culture, no one is certain that the leader in charge will stay the course on a transformation agenda. Typically, a history of half-baked and half-hearted change programs undermines confidence that the current challenge will be treated any differently. Without a clear vision and definite commitment from above, even the most capable and energetic members of the leadership team will hesitate to raise new ideas for moving forward – and the less-proven executives will feel even more reluctant to speak their minds about what is wrong and how to improve things.

Successful transformations call for a rigorous confrontation of reality, both external and internal. But all that work will be wasted if the leader hasn't paused to establish that all executives must help chart the new course. Every member of your management team must understand the requirement to take an active role – no exceptions. If you permit wallflowers during the planning phase, they are likely to cast long, passive shadows over their part of the organization when it comes time for execution.

Beyond mandating involvement, you have to provide *safe passage* – enable managers and employees to be brutally honest about what they see as the company's greatest weaknesses and encourage them to contribute ideas on how to launch the transformation and keep it going. You can start by getting the leadership team to agree on a simple set of ground rules for discussing ideas, engaging in critical thinking, and making decisions. (More on this is given in Chapter 5.) Be ready to enforce them because team members are likely to revert to their old ways if you don't.

Next, clearly spell out how everyone in the organization will move from the current state to the desired new state. You must describe the major steps and deliverables in your launch process as well as how and when people at different levels in the company will become engaged in the transformation launch and journey.

After that, have an objective third party conduct a round of interviews with key leaders about what's working or not working and what's the best way to proceed. Guarantee anonymity, and assemble the findings in an unattributed, verbatim fashion. In addition, gather fact-based insights from inside and outside the organization to test the assumptions underlying your new success model.

Once you've completed those tasks, convene a well-designed *Confronting Reality* event so that you and your team can work your way through all of the new information to develop and refine the purpose, strategic vision, and supporting success model. And then road test everything before drawing conclusions and finalizing the transformation plan.

The aforementioned steps will enable you to quickly address important issues and make difficult resource-allocation decisions. By avoiding a false start with your management team, you won't have to revisit strategic questions, redo key elements of your business model, or reprioritize initiatives – all of which would bog down your launch and sap energy from execution.

ACCELERATOR #2: THE "NO-SLACK" LAUNCH

In most cases, the day-to-day management process is already operating at full capacity when the firm's leaders sound the call for a big change. There isn't room within the established system to plan and launch a transformation – in fact, they often get in the way. Forcing the launch process into the organization's preexisting calendar of meetings will give short shrift to this important work and not allow adequate time for the structured dialogue that's so essential to breaking new ground.

The solution is to create a turbocharged, *No-Slack Launch* process that runs on a separate track and promotes both high speed and high engagement. Running a No-Slack Launch alongside the routine management process for a few months will enable you to accelerate the transformation, gaining not only precious time but also energy, commitment, and momentum.

A peek at this turbocharged overlay to the day-to-day management process is shown below. This process architecture will be developed in detail later; but for now, it is important to make note of the greatly shortened time frame along the bottom of the illustration and the overall compression into very few essential steps (Exhibit 2.2).

You'll need to lay out for the management team, and then for all employees, a *roadmap* with specific waypoints and dates. The roadmap must be *sparse* even though it must extend with the main event dates out beyond the launch phase through the end of the first full performance year. It's a good idea to refer to the Re-plan Phase at year end. This signals that you mean business and helps everyone get over the "this too will pass" thought process. The sparseness of the roadmap will also signal that the extra work on transformation is well conceived and packaged and will not amount to a waste of everyone's time.

With proper preparation and good design, your team and the third-tier leaders reporting directly to it should go from confronting reality to finalizing initiatives in three to four meetings, interspersed with prework, testing, and refinements. The accompanying schedule must be highly compressed. *If team members feel they don't have quite enough time, you probably have it about right.* When people receive a few extra weeks to complete a step, they often wait until the last week or so to bear down. Just a few extensions can balloon a three-month launch phase into six months or even a year.

All members of the Senior Leadership Team reporting to the Transformation Leader should each be asked to help craft one of the transformation initiatives and later to oversee its execution companywide. Preferably, each Transformation Initiative should be assigned two co-champions: one senior line executive and one senior functional staff leader. They will perform these cross-organizational duties in addition to being responsible for their own departments' progress on all transformation initiatives. By wearing both hats, senior team leaders will greatly increase the transformation's traction. It is important to give every member of the senior leadership team a transformation job in addition to their routine line or staff duty.

The No-Slack Launch stands in stark contrast to the counsel that everything must be perfectly prepared ahead of time, with troves of analyzed data, a completely articulated strategy and new success model, and all the right people in the right positions. Many Transformation Leaders who follow that advice find themselves shunted onto the sidetracks, still waiting to fire up their engine as the market roars by and valuable employees leave to find better vehicles to advance their careers. *Preparation is important, but not at the expense of motion.* And motion is critical because it allows you to accrue small victories that entice the undecided to come on board. To this end, I often recommend that the senior leadership team identify during their first planning meeting and pursue a few visible "Quick Starts" that can be accomplished even before the major transformation initiatives have been detailed and are ready to launch.

Perhaps the most important reason to get moving is that every day of action accelerates the cycle of organizational learning and adaptation. The moment a solution is envisioned, put it into play. If it proves to be faulty, quickly drop it – and chalk it up as a lesson to apply to your transforming business.

EXHIBIT 2.2   The No-Slack Launch

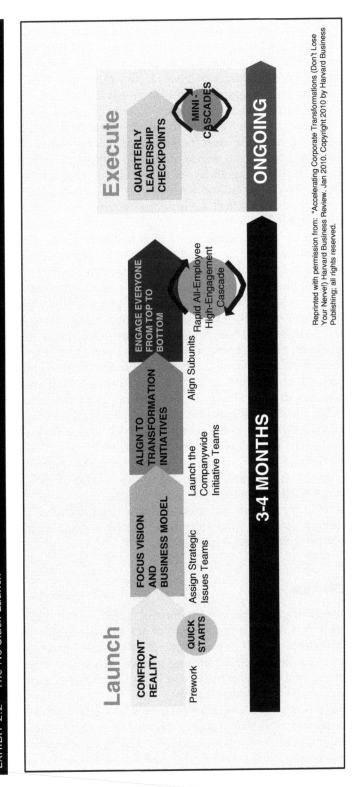

EXHIBIT 2.2   The No-Slack Launch

ACCELERATOR #3: DELIBERATELY COMPRESSED AGENDA

Transformation Leaders may lack the insight and courage to discard efforts that have come up short. A common fear is that if they admit they've chosen a wrong path or gotten the timing wrong, they will lose their ability to motivate the team to try other things. So instead, they pile big, new initiatives on top of the ones that are struggling – and the result is gridlock.

Initiative gridlock often starts simply, innocuously. Suppose that Finance puts new tools in place to better control overhead costs. And then Human Resources introduces a new employee performance management system to better identify top contributors. Marketing initiates a campaign to boost sales of new products. Manufacturing kicks off a Six Sigma program that will eventually touch Marketing, Sales, and Finance. Also, the top executive team embarks on a culture-change effort to improve morale and retention (ironically, the low morale stems from too many initiatives overloading the system and the people). Individually, each project makes sense, but when launched simultaneously, with no regard for strategic alignment or prioritization, these multiple layers of activity easily overwhelm the organization.

One example at the start of a global retailer's transformation launch comes to mind. We were extending our discovery process when we interviewed a field manager who introduced us to the unwritten "Two Drawer Method," he and his colleagues had devised for responding to the relentless to-dos they received from well-intentioned functional executives above them in the chain of command. This shared survival technique involved taking all new memos received in the field regarding new corporate initiatives and putting them in a desk drawer. If anyone followed up on a particular memo, it was pulled out of the drawer, considered a "real priority," and tagged for some sort of action. At the end of the month, if nobody called on the rest of the memos, the stack of memos was moved to a second drawer. After two months, if nobody called to follow up about any of those memos in the second drawer, it was okay to throw them away. At the end of each month, the rolling two-month file ultimately got thrown away!

Executives who try to stuff too much into the organizational pipeline will clog it. Workers' capacity to execute will become a choke point if the programs are not prioritized and sequenced.

Doing More ON Less

The best response is *triage*. In the most successful corporate transformations, managers restrict their action agendas to three, or at most four, well-articulated companywide initiatives – each one containing only two or three carefully selected areas of focus tied to clear outcome metrics. When you start multiplying the initiatives by the areas of focus, you'll quickly realize that exceeding this guideline will gridlock the organization.

For example, a new CEO's first order of business at a global retailer was to disband 1,000 teams, and work with a largely inherited senior leadership team to distill three critical initiatives from all the complexity. Having to oversee and guide the work of so many teams, the previous CEO had led the whole company into gridlock. When the new leader's compressed transformation agenda made it possible for everyone in the organization to focus time, attention, and resources on the turnaround, people were able to contribute much greater value to the effort. As a result, the retailer dramatically improved shareholder value, customer satisfaction, and employee retention by the end of the first year. If the transformation agenda hadn't been tightened, managers and employees would have been forced to develop their own ways of coping with directionless and oppressive gridlock.

Focus is not about doing more with less; it's about *doing more ON less*. Making choices about what not to do so that resources will go to the most important initiatives is not easy, but it must be done to overcome this embedded Inhibitor of your firm's transformation.

ACCELERATOR #4: COMMITTED AND CAPABLE CHANGE LEADERS

Protracted tolerance of recalcitrant team members, or of those who are unwilling or incapable of performing within the expectations of the transformation agenda, creates the necessity of another Accelerator. Many Transformation Leaders, even if they acknowledge this problem, choose to avoid conflict and hope that the clarity and efficacy of their grand plan will quickly win people over. And they're mostly right. After the top leader creates safe passage, establishes a reliable process architecture geared for speed and high engagement, and brings performance and behavior expectations into sharp focus, many team members will commit to the new transformation agenda.

But what do you do with the senior executives who do not come aboard? More important, how soon do you need to act? The simple answer is at this stage in your transformation launch, sooner rather than later. Remember, senior executives cast a large shadow sometimes over vast numbers of people in their part of the organization over which they hold sway. If it is clear at the start of transformation launch that especially a senior executive is firmly resisting coming aboard, it is best to confront that Inhibitor head on or run the risk that just one or two people will disrupt the speed of your organization's progress from planning to achieving breakthrough results. For others on the team, it may take engagement in your launch process, and the opportunity to air their own ideas in its deliberations before they can become fully committed. Just make sure all arrive at the starting gate of the cascade to all employees fully committed before you allow them to roll out your transformation game plan down through their parts of your organization.

The best approach is to quickly identify and confront executives who might undermine transformation. Even during the first few weeks of your launch, time compression helps to highlight three types of managers who could cause problems:

- *The quick adopters*, who jump aboard before they fully grasp what is involved and who view mastery of the new agenda as a springboard to success
- *The deniers*, who harbor a deep foreboding about being on the losing end of the inevitable power and resource shifts in a reinvention
- *The commitment averse*, who may not believe in your approach but remain on the fence, possibly because they see that the transformation is beginning to bear fruit

The more focused and explicit your launch process becomes, the easier it will be to identify the one or two members of the management team who could undermine the whole effort. Deal with those individuals first. That will send a strong signal to the other members of the team as well as to the rest of the organization that you mean business. Then you can coach people through the launch process to rise to the transformation challenge.

ACCELERATOR #5: TOP-TO-BOTTOM EMPLOYEE BUY-IN

Only after you have dealt with leaders who will not commit to the transformation can you attend to employee engagement and motivation.

Many transformation projects stall because the great ideas and strategies never make it far enough down in the organization to have an impact on the people who relate directly to customers or make the company's products. If you can't rapidly engage all employees and get them to commit to the agenda initiatives early on, the top team may move on to new challenges and strategies before your initial message reaches the full organization.

Most employee programs established to support a transformation aim to combine training and development with employee alignment and engagement during the launch period. Employee events during launch – often held off-site – usually take place over several days, sometimes a week or two. But such events won't do a bit of good if you (a) wait too long to hold them or (b) fail to engage and align employees from the outset.

A much better response is to deploy an Accelerator in the ACT Method called the *Rapid, High-engagement, All-employee Cascade™*. The experience of a major retailer, which took only a few weeks to engage and align its 40,000 employees around the world with its transformation plans and initiatives, is instructive. On the first day of the cascade, the regional vice presidents (executives three levels below the CEO who had been part of the intensive, three-month, No-Slack Launch) gathered in a room with their district managers. The major initiatives were presented, one at a time – and then the regional VPs, sitting at tables with their teams, shared the commitments they had made to drive each initiative before facilitating a discussion about how their district managers could contribute. At the end of the day, all participants turned in their preliminary commitments to action in their immediate areas of responsibility. Within one week, the district managers met with their regional VPs to finalize their commitments; a couple of weeks after that, they gathered for a day with all the store managers in their districts and went through the same process, which the store managers repeated with their teams. The cascade concluded with a three-hour companywide event early on a Sunday morning, right before doors opened to customers at all 800-plus stores.

Discussions were entirely devoted to rapidly engaging all levels of employees in the launch and establishing clear line-of-sight accountability for the major transformation initiatives from top to bottom. A conscious decision had been made to defer essential training and development until managers and employees were engaged and committed because then people would be better motivated to learn. The entire global high-engagement cascade took less than two months to complete.[3]

ACCELERATOR #6: ANTICIPATION OF EXECUTION "SLUMPS"

Once you have executives and employees on the road to transformation, it is important to keep them focused on the journey by setting concrete and visible intermediate goals. The last thing you need is an early chorus of "Are we there yet?" from the people who led the planning and launch phases. This is critical, because the more intensive and engaging the transformation launch, the harder it can be to sustain the heightened levels of energy, focus, and performance.

After working on alignment and commitment in the cascade sessions, people really do need to get down to the business of delivering on their commitments. Sometimes, the shift from planning to doing is mistaken as a departure from the big ideas that were the grist of the launch phase. As the day-to-day grind retakes center stage during the first quarter in the execution phase, old habits can gradually sneak up on the system. Leaders who had begun working in a more open and engaging way might switch back to command-and-control mode or turn their attention to other important activities. Priorities set in the launch phase will be challenged as people respond to more-immediate pressures to meet tactical goals.

You may begin to feel that you've done your part and that it is now time for the team to execute – but you must continue to *actively champion* the transformation initiatives by modeling the new desired behaviors. In addition, you must resist the temptation to constantly add new ideas to the mix to provoke or stimulate employees.

The transition from launch to execution is vulnerable to three predictable slumps. They cannot be completely avoided, but they are recognizable if you know where to look, and executive leaders and general managers can minimize their drag on the transformation effort. The moment you heard the words "Hey, we're over the hump," you are about to hit the first one. Here are some ways to work through them.

Postlaunch Blues

It can be tough for a leader to switch from playing a visionary role to serving as *"ballast and keel,"* but that is just what is needed after a strong launch because a real transformation is about execution. The top leader has to make sure managers at all levels receive and relay a consistent message about the need to drive the key transformation initiatives in the agreed-upon manner. One way to signal your shift into execution mode is to start weekly staff meetings with a review of progress on transformation initiatives, calling attention to people and plans that have drifted out of alignment and noting early lessons that need to be quickly shared. The same meeting reorientation needs to take place down through the organization.

Observable leadership behaviors such as this will renew faith that management is following through, build confidence that everyone is headed down the right path, and reinforce accountability to the commitments made during the planning. These behaviors will keep transformation energy high and everyone's focus where it needs to be.

Midcourse Overconfidence

The next major slump typically comes after two quarterly checkpoints have passed. The transformation initiatives are now well understood, and results have begun to register. A feeling of smooth sailing can set in.

You should not, however, turn on the autopilot. You will encounter unexpected execution challenges. The success model may need refining, and you will need to tweak initiatives based on lessons from early execution. As the excitement of the launch wears off, some executives may lobby for old, familiar methods that are more to their liking and better aligned with their existing skills. If you do not step up to affirm the commitments to transformation that have been so carefully put in place, other leaders may try to undo all the hard work that got everyone focused and moving down the new path.

One of your biggest midcourse challenges is to keep the transformation process focused, energized, and fresh. Beyond conducting a rigorous midcourse assessment of the transformation process itself, an effective way to increase both speed and traction is to hold *quarterly checkpoint meetings* that involve the top three levels of leaders and immediately follow each of them with *mini-cascades*, interventions that take place throughout the company.

Mini-cascades don't have to be expensive, time-consuming, overly produced events. In fact, it's better if they take only an hour or two each quarter and are folded right into regular operations. For instance, field supervisors on a construction site can chat with employees over coffee and donuts on the tailgate of a pickup truck before people start working. The important thing is to keep everyone, not just top executives, engaged and informed so they can make timely adjustments to accelerate progress in their scope of responsibility, and share in the transformation's success when it comes.

Presumed Perpetual Motion

As the first performance year comes to a close, many executives will succumb to the presumption of perpetual motion – the idea that things will continue to progress if the company simply sticks with the year-one game plan. You'll even hear a few executives say, "Let's not go through that again!" But the fact is that a fresh look at everything is necessary.

You'll need a *"launch redux"* to boldly kick off the second year of execution. Now that the organization has given the transformation initiatives an extended test drive, the leadership team should reexamine them and the thinking behind them, drawing on everyone's experience to make informed changes. Having been through all this before, the leadership team should be able to accomplish the launch redux in a rigorous but streamlined manner.

TOWARD A TRANSFORMATION GAME PLAN

Even one of the six Inhibitors can bring an entire transformation and all related breakthrough-performance aspirations to a sudden halt. Some of the Accelerators may seem counterintuitive. For instance, it might not be obvious at first how you can accelerate change by pausing to establish *safe passage* or setting time aside for *structured dialogue*, or how you can accomplish sweeping transformation by restricting your focus to a very few important initiatives. But the tactics discussed in this book will help you plan and execute a rapid organizational reinvention that actually sticks.

Now let's turn attention to the remainder of the book, which will reveal how these Inhibitor- and Accelerator-driven insights have been rolled up into a simple but comprehensive methodology; one that leaders facing very different challenges can deploy with their teams to orchestrate and achieve rapid transformation. The Accelerated Corporate Transformation metholody, or the "ACT Method" for short, has been developed over many years and many initiatives and challenges to enable leaders to routinely achieve rapid, system-wide transformation success.

TIPS FOR LEADING WITH ACCELERATORS

1. In developing your transformation game plan, make sure to include all six Accelerators. If you fail to identify, engage, and overcome even one of the embedded Inhibitors, you run the risk of derailing your transformation.

2. Make sure to take every opportunity to simplify your transformation game plan so that it minimally interferes with the necessary day-to-day management process and is easily understood by employees at all levels in the organization.

Notes

1. The discovery and initial articulation of the six Accelerators to rapid, organization-wide transformation were first revealed in Robert H. Miles, "Accelerating Corporate Transformations: Don't Lose Your Nerve!" Harvard Business Review, January–February 2010. This chapter expands on the meaning of the "Accelerators" and the role they play in transformation leadership. Reprinted with permission from Harvard Business Press. Copyright 2010 by Harvard Business Publishing; all rights reserved.

2. Robert H. Miles, Corporate Comeback: The Story of Renewal and Transformation at National Semiconductor. San Francisco: Jossey-Bass Publications, a division of John Wiley & Sons, 1997.

3. Robert H. Miles, "Beyond the Age of Dilbert: Accelerating Corporate Transformations by Rapidly Engaging All Employees," Organizational Dynamics, 2001, Vol. 29, No. 4, pp. 313–321.

CHAPTER 3

Accelerated Corporate Transformation
The Foundations

"The most profound attributes that set ACT apart are its leader-led-at-all-levels mandate, its unique cascade method for quickly engaging all employees, and its speed to breakthrough results, based on simplicity or economy of concepts and compression of processes."

The antidotes to the inhibitors of rapid transformation are the *accelerators* available to Transformation Leaders in the Accelerated Corporate Transformation, or ACT, process architecture. ACT makes it possible for leaders at all levels to execute rapid, large-scale transformations, while at the same time delivering short-term results every day. As you will soon see in the stories that follow, transformations usually boil down to "a few well-articulated initiatives targeted for breakthrough results in a short period of time … in a sea of necessary incremental improvements" (Exhibit 3.1).[1]

Achieving this balance is one of the most difficult challenges you will face as a Transformation Leader and one of the most rewarding when you get it right. But this challenge has become more acute than before imagined. It used to be generally recognized most high-achieving executive leaders got to rise to a transformation challenge at most only once in a career. With little practice beforehand, the odds of success in these previously uncharted waters were let's say, less than hoped; and in today's fast-paced, disruptive environment, much worse. Those who could pull off such a feat became the CEO icons of their age.

Today's universal compression of cycle time across almost all industries and sectors is creating waves of transformation challenges in rapid succession that have had two major consequences for the guidance available to executive leaders to ensure success. Even industries previously insulated from big swings in fortune have had to yield to the speedup and compression of many aspects of their systems as a derivative of the march of new technology.

DOI: 10.4324/9781003272724-3

EXHIBIT 3.1   The Accelerators in the ACT Method

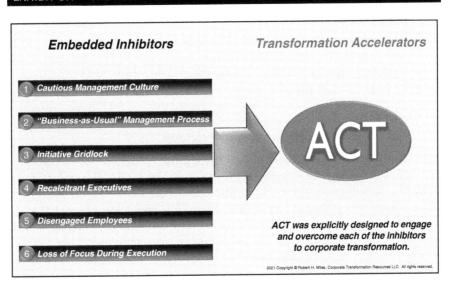

Embedded Inhibitors   *Transformation Accelerators*

1 *Cautious Management Culture*

2 *"Business-as-Usual" Management Process*

3 *Initiative Gridlock*

4 *Recalcitrant Executives*

5 *Disengaged Employees*

6 *Loss of Focus During Execution*

ACT was explicitly designed to engage and overcome each of the inhibitors to corporate transformation.

First, the speed with which transformation must achieve breakthrough success has greatly accelerated. Put simply, transformations must be both bold and rapid to be successful. There's no time to dither at the starting gate.

Second, the compression of successive waves of potentially disruptive competitive forces has created an environment in which organizations must build the competence for leading transformations deeply into the marrow of their management process. Indeed, as I write this book, a worldwide pandemic is raging; one that is dramatically raising the demand for leaders possessing the methodology and unique skills for quickly transforming all types of organizations once the alarm is off. Fledging firms before the outbreak of the virus and global sequester, whose success models align well with social distancing – think streaming video, arm's length delivery, interactive electronic gaming, and social media of all stripes – have become overnight growth rockets, while many of the corporate blue bloods are being brought to their knees. One group will have to transform to keep up with their new opportunities, while the other will have to quickly reinvent their prosperity.

Where once it was sufficient to transform something to a target future state, now that once-acquired transformational competence must be enabled to permeate the entire enterprise to make it continuously agile in anticipating and adapting to new challenges. Because an ACT-guided transformation is led by leaders at all levels in the organization, with staff and consultants playing support roles, such leaders acquire and practice the valuable new skills and competencies, which do not leave the premises with outside advisors when the project is over.

Transformation has been used to describe everything from high-risk overhauls of a business to tactical changes in IT systems. So, to be clear, *transformation* applies to a wide range of institutional challenges. The typical range of client transformation challenges that served over the years as anvils for sculpting and simplifying the ACT framework included the following:

- New executive leader's "taking charge" process to engage all levels in the organization in a bold new transformation agenda and success model
- Sitting executive leader's need to launch the next major phase in the organization or major component of it
- Bold and rapid pivot to a major new strategy and set of initiatives
- Re-alignment of people, process, and technology initiatives with a new purpose, strategic vision, and success model – a total system redo
- Post-merger integration of executive leadership, organization structure and systems, success models, and cultures

This is tough work, and most efforts fall short.

How have we been faring with these challenges? Not great. Based on data from a poll of 11,000 workers, fewer than half of employees understand their company's strategic goals, less than 25% feel their organization sets goals that people are enthusiastic about, only *38%* believe their planning results in clear assignments for individuals, and 43% feel there isn't any follow-through on the plans anyway. Not a fertile field upon which to nurture a major transformation.[2]

TACTICAL IS NOT TRANSFORMATIVE

The range of methods for attempting to lead transformations is as varied as transformation challenges themselves. Some leaders resort to dramatic communication campaigns, believing that if people can just "get it," they *will* "get on with it." Others attempt to grease the skids of a transformation launch with a barrage of tactical change management, corporate communications, and employee training interventions. Some quickly turn their transformation over to program management offices populated by external consultants and then move on to other issues. Still other leaders, scorecard everything in sight, because of their gut belief in measurement and delegation.

Clearly, each of these and many other management orthodoxies contain elements that can contribute to transformation success, that is, if they are tightly aligned with the critical path of the transformation. But none of these more operational and tactical approaches were designed from the outset to handle all the *inhibitors* and unleash all their *accelerators* as well as all the moving parts in an enterprise-wide, top-to-bottom, transformation. However, within the orchestration of a proven transformation game plan, many of these tactical methodologies can play an important supporting role; again, as long as they take their lead from the transformation game plan and roadmap I am about to introduce. Similarly, many of the more contemporary tactical tools – social media schemes, for example – can play a major role downstream in a corporate transformation, but too much of this good thing during the early alignment and engagement phases of transformation launch generally creates a false sense understanding of the transformation constructs and superficial commitment to them. More about this in the following chapters, especially on the Align and Cascade phases.

So, how can you lay out a transformation game plan up front that allows everyone to understand, relate, and commit to performing his or her role in an aligned and energetic manner? How can you orchestrate a leader-led transformation? One that benefits from the best talents and support from your internal staff departments? And how can you sustain the early high level of energy and focus throughout the Execute Phase?

There's a better way.

GET YOUR ACT TOGETHER

The value proposition for ACT has been the same for many years:

> *ACT is a proven, enterprise-level process architecture. It enables a Transformation Leader to rapidly orchestrate the launch of the next major phase in his or her organization in a simple, high-engagement manner to achieve breakthrough results.*

Over the years, countless leaders and teams have leveraged the same implementation process, and ACT has been refined and streamlined with their contributions. The speed to breakthrough results and the intensity of employee engagement achieved and sustained are well documented and have been widely shared, especially in the business community. By focusing the responsibility for leading the transformation squarely in the hands of leaders at all levels, ACT-based transformations also leave in their wake palpable, hard to achieve improvements in leadership skills and organizational culture.

Following are three examples of the dramatic shifts in performance that are possible, even at a very large scale, within a single performance year (not years). The companies profiled implemented the ACT process to quickly generate their breakthrough results.

In contrast to the typical, failed transformation launch illustrated in the Preface, these successful efforts looked like the curves shown in Exhibit 3.2

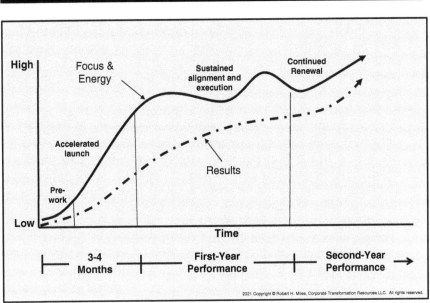

EXHIBIT 3.2   Typical ACT-Based Transformation Launch

where focus and energy were built early and then sustained, leading to compounding growth in results at a very large scale.

- **Restoring Shareholder Value at a Global Retailer:** Twelve months after it failed to merge with a major competitor, the new, internally promoted CEO of a major global retailer faced a huge challenge: to rapidly revitalize the company's sagging retail operations. The firm's leaders resolved to once again make the company the industry's most compelling place to *invest, shop,* and *work.* Indeed, these became the major transformation initiatives upon which the company's revitalization was launched. They succeeded. In one year, the company's share price jumped by 156%, customer complaints fell by 50%, and employee retention rates rose by 72%. The company also moved up from the bottom 10% of the Standard & Poor's 500 to number two in terms of percentage increase in shareholder value. *"The biggest surprise,"* the CEO reflected, *"was how quickly people in our company said, 'Count me in. Let's go.' I knew it would happen; I just didn't think we'd get there this fast."*[3]
- **Restructuring for Dramatic Cost Improvement in America's Most Admired Utility:** One of the largest electric utilities in the U.S. needed to transform its major production function, which consisted of fossil fuel and hydroelectric power plants spread over several geographically dispersed operating companies, each with its own union, into a single, new generation company (or GenCo). Changing from a confederation of line units within a regulated public utility into a self-contained, competitive business required the GenCo to learn a whole new way of thinking and acting, all under the white-hot light of a nationally prominent parent company that was acclaimed as *Fortune* magazine's "Most Admired" company in the utility industry and was the nation's largest power company at the time. Referred to as the "Low Cost = Job Security" transformation in the vast Fossil/Hydro generation operation, the makeover involved almost 100 plants and dams and over 50,000 union-based employees reporting to several separate subsidiaries, and the feat was accomplished in the middle of a CEO transition. After the repositioning, the company's operating costs were reduced by more than $100 million in a year and over $300 million in three years, while accidents were cut by 30% and union grievances fell by 72%. Employee morale leaped as well.[4]
- **Restoration of Rapid Growth in a Silicon Valley High-Tech Icon**: Once a vibrant Silicon Valley high-tech company, a global high-tech software leader, had stopped growing. Sales had stagnated at a little less than a half billion per year, largely because its past strategy of acquiring companies for growth had run its full course. In fact, all the best targets in the market had been acquired, and future growth would require a different strategy based on internal innovations. With strong leadership and the simple ACT-based transformation process, this software leader managed to fold its disconnected subsidiaries into one smoothly integrated business focused on customer needs. The new customer focus and highly engaged team revived innovation, inspired new products, and triggered steady sales growth worldwide. In the first

year alone, the company improved morale, slashing employee turnover by 41%, while its stock price rose by 53%, its revenue jumped by 24%, and its profitability soared by 290%.[5]

Note that in addition to breakthrough results, these ACT-based transformation projects also generated major improvements in management acumen and organization culture, again by the end of the first year of execution, in large measure because of the intensive Launch Phase all employees went through.

To reliably achieve these transformational results, it is critical to recognize as the Transformation Leader that *all* the *few* steps in the rapid, simple ACT launch process count. They serve as the accelerators needed to overcome the embedded inhibitors in a transforming organization.

I will refer back to these case examples several times in the book to illustrate key ACT concepts.

THE ACT BASICS

The surprisingly simple ACT-based process architecture contains the foundational elements for simply and reliably engaging and overcoming the "inhibitors," which is essential to achieving a rapid and successful transformation.

Let's take a closer look at ACT.

The ACT process itself does not look too different on the surface. Many people sharing advice and methodologies have roadmaps that will look almost identical to the untrained eye. However, there are big differences when you go to deploy them. As my former colleague and coauthor, Michael Kanazawa, also a musician, once observed,

> Just as two pieces of music can look very similar on paper, one creates beauty when played, and the other creates dissonant noise. On the surface, both scores will have notes, bars, and markings that are the basics of music. But if the notes aren't in the correct sequence and timing and played in the correct key and note combinations, it will just produce noise.

The most profound attributes that set ACT apart are its leader-led-at-all-levels mandate, its unique cascade method for quickly engaging all employees, and its speed to breakthrough results, based on simplicity or economy of concepts and compression of processes. Please hold these pillar differentiators of ACT as you work through the remaining chapters which follow the transformation roadmap from start to finish.

For the moment, however, just consider the ACT-based architecture a symphony that has continuously been played through, improved, and boiled down to the essentials over years of productive work and active use. Each time a new leader uses it, he or she turns another crank on streamlining, a process that's been going through refinement for over 30 years. So, the fact that it is simple and not some Rube Goldberg type of contraption with lots of extra moving parts is intentional and took hard work. Each part has been simplified, compressed, and optimally sequenced; it plays off the other parts in an intentional way in which you as a Transformation Leader can depend. Moreover, this implementation methodology is perfectly horizontal. It has never met an industry vertical or sector in which it failed to succeed. It is

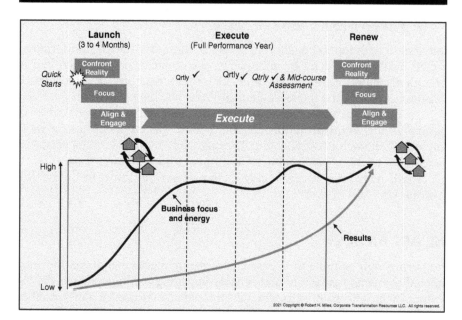

EXHIBIT 3.3   ACT Process Architecture

worth noting that several CEOs have deployed ACT in the transformation of several enterprises, each facing a very different transformation challenge.

In its simplest expression, the *Accelerated Corporate Transformation,* or *ACT*, process architecture takes the form illustrated in Exhibit 3.3. The highlighted elements are the *foundational* elements that are necessary for effectively leading an accelerated transformation.

ACT AND *PRODUCTIVE* SPEED

The basic ACT-based plan starts with the Launch Phase, compressed into three, no more than four months, that goes from confronting reality, clarifying the purpose, strategic vision, success model, company values, corporate transformation initiatives, as well as some obvious "Quick Starts" to get the process moving while planning proceeds. The Launch is an accelerated overlay to the regular management process. It consists of a series of compressed Launch Phases, before shifting into the Execute Phase.

By my count, the Launch Phase consists of two to three 1-1/2 day gatherings of the Senior Leadership Team (the SLT, consisting of the Transformation Leader and his or her direct reports) and two larger gatherings of the Extended Leadership Team (the ELT, which adds the SLTs' direct reports). In fact, the second meeting of the ELT actually kicks off the Cascade Phase. It lasts for only three to four months. I cannot remember when a leadership team felt the need to tack on another major event during the Launch Phase.

Think for a moment. *This is what is meant by ACT's speed through simplification and compression of transformation content and process.*

Then the Cascade Phase rapidly engages the full organization – in a matter of weeks to a couple of months, depending on the organization's size and geographical dispersion – which enables and engages managers and employees at all levels to translate the organization's transformation constructs into individual commitments to action that are relevant for their level and job scope. ACT accomplishes this rollout with its unique *Rapid, High-Engagement, All-Employee Cascade*™ methodology and tools. Again, speed is based on simplification and compression, which comes from repeated ACT projects across a great variety of transformation challenges and sectors. More on the nature and pervasiveness of speed in transformation work – called *Productive Speed* – will be articulated in the next chapter. It lies at the core of the structure and process of ACT-based interventions.

The cascade is followed by a longer Execute Phase that puts in place quarterly leadership performance checkpoints to hold accountabilities, share leading practices across the divisions and departments, and make mid-course adjustments in an agile way when needed. Each quarterly checkpoint is quickly followed by a mini cascade that enables managers and employees in all organizational components to gauge their progress on the transformation initiatives and make timely refinements in their commitments to further accelerate their part of the transformation.

Finally, there is a Renew Phase at the end of the first performance year under ACT, which is designed to refresh the major (max of 3 to 4) transformation initiatives in light of actual achievements and associated organizational learning. This phase re-engages *everyone* in a relaunch of the ACT-based transformation process, although in a more streamlined manner than was possible the first time through.

The top of Exhibit 3.3 shows a skeleton of the full process architecture; the bottom of the figure shows that organizational energy is built and sustained over time. Note that the process steps are designed and sequenced specifically to maintain the performance focus and energy to drive results over the course of the first full performance cycle following the cascade to all employees, usually one year. When implemented in a particular manner without skipping any of its few simple steps, the ACT process creates energy and momentum, as well as an acceleration of performance and culture change as it becomes gradually integrated into the management process. Importantly, every step at every level is leader-led.

The book would end here were it not for the sustained transformation leadership and all the "in between" work that must be done to make the key events on the ACT roadmap powerful and replace all the complexity with simplicity through compression of steps and processes. These elements of ACT will be the focus of the rest of the book.

CREATING SAFE PASSAGE

Before leaving this introduction to ACT, it is important to highlight its first step, "creating safe passage." Because of its centrality in the ACT process, we will also return to it later. But for now.

The first key to effectively launching a tight transformation game plan is to make sure that everyone understands the path that will be followed and how and where they fit in. It is fun to say that "we need a burning platform" to get people moving. Sounds decisive. You might get people scrambling out of concern or fear, but that is not the kind of energy you need to create to be successful in leading a transformation.

Before launching your transformation, you need to make sure that there is a clear and *safe passage* from the state of things today to the intended new state or strategic direction. Safe passage does not mean that 100% of the people will keep their jobs or that all budgets will remain intact. Everyone knows and understands the realities of making difficult trade-offs to refocus an organization. So, above all, be honest if there are these types of tough decisions that will need to be made. What is expected by your team is that you lay out a very clear process architecture that shows a few critical steps: who will make decisions, when and how people will have input into the decisions, when you will announce final answers, and what will happen as these decisions are made.

There is one qualifier to the term "safe passage" from the perspective of motivating a whole organization to drive the effort. It is not sufficient to simply lay out your process in advance. Your process needs to be specifically designed for speed and high engagement to be received well and to work. In addition, a transformation often creates an opportunity to set a purposeful "burning ambition" as the motivator to change; a compelling shared purpose and reason for being that truly energizes employees and hastens progress down the critical path to the desired future state.

Many processes don't have both the speed and high-engagement elements covered. The typical belief is that to get speed, you can't spend time on soft things like employee involvement, engagement, and dialogue. While under the gun by a board or boss to quickly focus an organization on a new strategic path, it can seem too messy and time consuming to get too many people involved. However, to generate a burning ambition in the team necessary to engage fully and continue driving the transformation, the right kind of people investments up front is required. Strategy is not done by consensus, that's true, but it can be done quickly with high engagement. As is typically the case with shortcuts like speeding past engaging the right people up front, things end up taking longer because of repeated revisits to past decisions, continued questioning, lack of alignment, and rework.

JUST A BETTER WAY OF MANAGING

One parting word of caution on launching this type of process. It is generally necessary to provide an overview of ACT at the beginning of engagement with each level of employees. That seems to be sufficient aside from reminding people of when they gather where they stand in terms of waypoints on the transformation roadmap. But ACT is intuitive enough that it doesn't require its own center stage to become operational. As one Transformation Leader of an ACT-based project once reflected,

So many other times we would launch programs that were extraneous to our regular jobs. And those other programs were focused just on the executive team. We would come back from one of those off-sites, and everyone on the team would be looking at us suspiciously and questioningly, like 'OK, just tell me what you want me to do now.' With an effective transformation process like ACT, it is not a program. It just becomes the way the business is managed. The process just became our normal management practice as a part of daily life from setting strategy to setting individual personal business commitments and following through on performance.

Similarly, another seasoned CEO of technology startups as well as large companies pointed out following his ACT-based intervention that,

Our transformation process was all about taking charge of our future. The process was an opportunity to look at the business as a whole and ask really tough questions. Instead of defending the status quo, it was more about understanding where the world was going. This type of effort has to be a formal process; otherwise, you won't make the time to address it or the conditions for people to be open minded and self-critical, which are necessary components.

With this brief overview of the ACT process architecture, and its opening introductions to "productive speed" and "creating safe passage," the bulk of the subsequent chapters pace you through the transformation roadmap, stopping at each major phase of this approach to rapid transformation. Each chapter reveals what you need to do to successfully lead your transformation as it unfolds, one phase at a time.

We call these ACT steps the *foundations* of transformation – those few, but essential steps that all Transformation Leaders must master for success. They contain the *accelerators* that enable you to identify, engage, and overcome the *inhibitors* of rapid transformation.

TIPS FOR PLANNING YOUR ACCELERATED TRANSFORMATION

- Follow a simple, streamlined process that starts with the creation of "safe passage" for the ELT. Don't be tempted to skip an important step.
- Begin with a clear framework and roadmap in place that shows how and when people will become engaged, and decisions will be made.
- Leverage a proven transformation process architecture and customize it for your situation.
- Be principally guided by an emphasis on simplicity of content and compression in process. In transformation work, this kind of speed – productive speed – is your best friend.
- Treat your approach to corporate transformation as simply how your organization will eventually be managed; anticipate and encourage the gradual melding of your transformation process with your management.

Notes

1. This chapter draws from and expands on the author's previous work on the ACT Methodology in Robert H. Miles, Leading Corporate Transformation: A Blueprint for Business Renewal. San Francisco: Jossey-Bass Publishers, a division of John Wiley & Sons, 1997 and Robert H. Miles and Michael Kanazawa, BIG Ideas to BIG Results: Accelerating Corporate Transformation in a Disruptive World, Second Edition, Pearson, 2016.

2. Harris Interactive survey of 11,000 U.S. workers.

3. Brian O'Connor, "Anatomy of a Turnaround: How Bruce Nelson Revived Office Depot," Fasttrack Magazine, April 2002, pp. 42–48.

4. Robert H. Miles, "Type I Transformation: Repositioning America's Most Admired Utility," Leading Corporate Transformation: A Blueprint for Business Renewal. San Francisco: Jossey-Bass Publishers, a division of John Wiley & Sons, 1997, pp. 83–126.

5. Robert H. Miles and Michael Kanazawa, BIG Ideas to BIG Results: Accelerating Corporate Transformation in a Disruptive World, Second Edition, Pearson, 2016, pp. 10–11.

CHAPTER 4

Structuring Your Transformation Launch

Productive Speed = Simplicity x Compression

At the first moment during Launch, the leader of a transformation not only has the greatest ability to shape the design of the whole effort but also to permanently imprint the culture and management process of the whole enterprise.[1] Just as organizations become imprinted with certain indelible characteristics at the time of their founding, so too do they become demonstrably reshaped in enduring ways by the manner their transformations are launched.[2]

All successful transformations must embrace a *structure* or architecture that is remarkably simple and is geared for speed and engagement. They must deploy a *process* that is designed to "create safe passage" for everyone participating. In an ACT-based transformation that should mean everyone in the organization. These structure and process elements comprise the yin and yang of successful, enterprise-wide transformations.

IMPRINTING YOUR ORGANIZATION

The imprinting of the organization as envisioned in the transformation game plan starts at Launch during the very first meeting of the Transformation Leader and the *Senior Leadership Team (SLT)*, and it quickly extends to the third tier of corporate leadership, the *Extended Leadership Team (ELT)*, which is made up of the teams that lead all of the business or line units and staff departments. By the time the Cascade Phase is completed, everyone in the enterprise is involved, engaged, and committed through immersion in the same corporate transformation game plan, structure, and process that their leaders went through. Moreover, the essence of the ACT-based approach to transformation is eventually absorbed into the day-to-day and year-to-year management process, enabling the enterprise to become progressively more proactive, aligned, and agile as new transformation challenges and opportunities continue to arise.

DOI: 10.4324/9781003272724-4

To help you see the important and complementary elements of the ACT-based transformation *structure* and *process*, we need to separate them in this and the next chapter. But let's be clear: in the life of the enterprise-wide transformation, these essential elements of successful rapid transformations are both mutually reinforcing and inextricable.

Based on decades of refinement from an intensive corporate transformation practice, ACT clearly represents the simplicity on the other side of transformation complexity. After you see what the essential core ACT elements are – in terms of both *structure* and *process* – you must be careful not to heap on too many other "good ideas," many from well-intentioned managers and staff professionals. Be parsimonious during your transformation Launch. Add to the steps managers and employees must take only those that are absolutely on the transformation critical path and in keeping with the rapid tempo. Otherwise, you will dampen the speed on which successful transformations depend and encumber everyone.

STRUCTURING RAPID TRANSFORMATIONS

From the structural perspective, we need to breathe life into six design elements: (1) the overall ACT architecture, including its framework and the all-important transformation Roadmap; (2) Productive Speed, the core ACT discipline; (3) the "No-Slack" Launch, the crucible of transformation; (4) the companywide Transformation Initiative Teams; (5) the Transformation Process Support Team; and (6) "Quick Starts." As you will see, the manner in which the Launch Phase is structured soon sets the template for the cascade to every component, level, and employee in the organization.

Full treatment of the *process* elements, which focus largely on rapidly creating energy, engagement, commitment, and accountability, will be deferred until the next chapter. And throughout both Launch chapters will be laced the *speed imperative* at the heart of the ACT-based approach.

Speed permeates everything in an ACT-based transformation game plan. Indeed, it is the first name in this approach to transformation. So, let's digress for a moment to articulate why speed is so important to Transformation Leaders, and what we mean by speed in this context, before coming back to the core elements of the ACT process architecture.

SPEED: A CORE ACT DISCIPLINE

Transformation Leaders achieve *Productive Speed* by *simplifying* the transformation constructs and *compressing* its steps. Unproductive speed, in contrast, often results when a leader commits errors of omission in the design of the transformation game plan, skips an essential step in the Roadmap, or rushes through deliberations without structuring them to ensure efficient, high-quality dialogue. Often this occurs because the leader simply desires speed for its own sake or because of the feeling of being under the gun to make something happen. So, it's important to pause here to take a closer look at the meaning of the speed dimension in leading transformations.

To put a large organization in motion, what matters is to get the train moving the right way down the right set of tracks quickly. When that happens, you will be truly surprised to see how many people climb aboard before it leaves the station! The right people will get on right away. Those who want to make the trip but were thinking they might be able to postpone it until a more convenient time will step on as well to see how things unfold during the first few stops ahead. Those who are uncertain about whether they want to go in the new direction will have to make up their minds. At some of the next few stops, some will get off because, after a closer look, they've changed their minds!

Forward motion gets both intellectual and emotional attention. In one sweep, it signals intention, purpose, and commitment, as well as the direction in which the organization is laying its new tracks.

Speed is a key enabler of success in transformations and strategic shifts. But it has to be the right kind and pace of speed. Productive Speed reinforces decisive action, which helps generate interest and energy and accelerates the realization of early returns and, ultimately, breakthrough results. Unproductive speed shows up as frantic flailing, lots of skipped steps that produce a lot of activity, but no breakthrough results.

There is a balancing point in all of this. But the average leadership team spends far too little time in preparing to run at top speed; hence, they operate handicapped, running at a frantic pace with a lot of wasted energy. A retail senior executive who was an ACT client was challenged with running his team like a start-up within a global multibillion-dollar company. He explained the need for speed to his team this way:

> *Speed is a choice, and it is a competitive advantage. A transformation process provides a vehicle to accelerate change. It can be a ritual like a pre-shot routine, not a rut.*

The reason results get better is that speed reduces unproductive dithering; it doesn't allow time for protracted dysfunctional political posturing. It avoids overanalyzing and, more important, overengineering solutions. It shifts the emphasis to a learning-from-doing mode, which enables leaders to achieve results and continue building on that success to reach even loftier goals. But the speed imperative in transformation work emerged from a host of other reasons as well.

The Need for Speed

Getting to breakthrough results faster is, of course, the major goal of accelerating a transformation process. As you increase the pace, shorten the decision cycles, and accelerate the alignment and engagement processes, the greater your results will be. Eventually, there might be some natural limits to these effects of increased speed. It's just that I have not encountered them yet!

Not long ago it was believed that strategic plans should be the span of a typical CEO's tenure (during those days) and that it would take multiple years to launch a transformation and turn an organization. But since then, many forces have conspired to dramatically accelerate the cycle times within organizations and the markets in which they compete. Perhaps the most profound and prolific influence on speed – the cycle time of execution – has been technology. As companies began to use an earlier version of the ACT methodology on the U.S. West Coast during the build out of the high-tech sector, the executives were quite appreciative of the tools for focused alignment and rigorous execution. ACT's simplicity was for them indeed on the other side of complexity.

The new wrinkle was that they all wanted to do these things in much less time. As they explained, the cycle time associated with their high-tech product development as well as the changing needs of their customers was a fraction of the big metal-bending and paper-pushing enterprises of the past. As time has progressed, another derivative phenomenon unfolded. The ultimate diffusion of high technology across all sectors has caused companies in all industries and of all shapes and sizes to become more capable of operating on a faster cycle. The "need for speed" has become ubiquitous across industries. The upgrades in the ACT methodology spawned by the high-tech sector have become useful to all industries, with fewer and lighter steps involving a more rapid launch pace to execution.

Other pervasive forces have also been at work reinforcing the need for speed. Not the least of which in the corporate arena has been the increasingly heavy push for takeovers. To put it bluntly, if you take too long to improve your business, an impatient activist investor just might get the job done for you! Rapidly expanding global competition, increasingly fickle customers, and just-in-time supply chain management are combining to drive the pace even faster today. To thrive and even survive today, executives need to be able to drive rapid cycles of improvement in their company strategies, success models, and operations.

All Aboard at Internet Speed

This brings us to the CEO of a successful technology company that hit a much-unexpected problem during the Internet boom. The CEO had transformed the company from a niche software player to the second-largest retail software vendor behind Microsoft. It was an exciting time.

Given all its success, it was hard to believe that the company was experiencing difficulties. But revenue growth had flattened, and several attempts to identify fast-growing businesses for acquisition had come up empty. As a result, the stock price had lost more than half of its value. Worse yet, the war for talent had start-ups enticing the company's star players with huge stock-option deals. Talented people were jumping off the train in growing numbers. Many literally jumped into BMW convertibles supplied by their new employers. Something had to be done, fast.

The CEO and his senior executives had an impressive track record. They had built companies from scratch, created breakthrough products, and led teams with a passion for new technologies. But the company now felt slow, plodding, and not very inventive.

Every day, the *San Jose Mercury News* profiled the latest wunderkinds. Fresh-faced engineering geniuses were ramping new businesses up and down Route 101. The CEO and his executives had no intention of sitting idly by, watching their company founder.

They began by confronting their current reality. The company had grown by acquiring software makers with strong products but poor distribution. Its solid relationship with retailers helped give a quick boost to the lagging sales of companies it acquired. But within a few years, though, few companies were left for the company to buy. Still the dominant player in its market, it lacked the means to jump-start growth. New markets had to be identified.

A separate problem revolved around the company's structure. It had developed into a loose collection of eight business units representing previously independent companies, each with its own product line. Little collaboration took place; in fact, the BUs often sniped at one another. To counter this feudal system, the company reorganized, coalescing into three highly focused, customer-centric business units. The three executives selected to run these units were chosen for their presumed ability to lead large, complex teams, generate growth, and boost new product development. Most important, they were viewed as both individual leaders and team players.

Obviously, the new arrangement left several of the old business unit heads out of key leadership positions. Some of them – former chief executives of acquired businesses – were more comfortable leading small teams with no corporate oversight. In short, they weren't the kind of general managers the company now needed, and they soon departed. To use the train analogy, the company was finally positioned on a specific track and was starting to move in the right direction. The "wrong people" knew it and got off the train just in time to allow for a smooth departure.

It was shortly after the reorganization that the CEO and his assembled new senior management team agreed on a strategic transformation. They agreed on a strategic transformation of the company using the ACT methodology. It would no longer focus on silo products; it would be a customer-driven company with the spotlight on solutions. To kick off the first year of the new company, they vowed that customer research would get as much attention as technology research. By understanding customer needs, the company would begin to create its own innovative products rather than just look for ways to acquire them. And while the market for retail software would remain a core piece of the business, growth would also come from moving into corporate markets. Above all, the leaders were compelled to become brutally honest about the challenges their organization faced. In the end, they embraced a plan to take the company down the track they had laid together. With growing enthusiasm, they urged managers to step forward and speed the train to the next destination. They named their corporate transformation process "Taking Charge."

The corporate transformation game plan put the company on a new path that kept gifted people in the company, eased out those who didn't fit into the new strategic plan, and attracted newcomers with more of the right talents. Within two years, the shift toward retail focus to corporate customers had become a significant part of the company's business.

Moral to the story? The most important reason to get moving is that every day of action accelerates the cycle of organizational learning and adaptation. Movement starts the learning process that must precede any necessary adjustments and refinements, which, in turn, increases your chances of besting your competitors. Cultures that are focused on execution aren't likely to let problems fester for years. In these cultures, the moment a solution is envisioned, it is put into play. If it proves to be faulty, it is just as quickly jettisoned and harvested for things learned to apply to the ongoing business.

In reflecting on the transformation experience of a global retailer, the president and COO recalled that one of the most important benefits was being able to see new leaders emerge from the ranks. Most of the executive team had tenures of 10–15 years, long by today's standards. The organization had struggled in recruiting outside talent and in making decisions about top team members who might not have been in the right roles for the new market requirements. But continued waiting to get the right people on board was not getting the team anywhere. They had to get the organization in motion, no more waiting.

As the company began to move from a pure operations focus to a market-centric approach, it became clearly uncomfortable for many of the leaders to make the shift. At the same time, natural leaders who had before not been exposed to the senior team in terms of their strategic thinking and leadership had the chance to interact more directly with the executives. Within the top three layers of management, individuals with talents in strategic planning, process design, and customer research began to shine. These were skills the company did not think it had, and it was a talent resource that was completely overlooked. By getting things in motion, these individuals were able to jump on board quickly, take leadership roles in helping the organization make the shift, and take the seats that others, by title, should have taken. For the president, the ability to get the transformation moving first and then use that motion to sort out the right people to keep was invaluable.

The Discipline of Productive Speed

Organizational speed is something that absolutely can and should be managed better. The keys to creating speed are counterintuitive to many leaders. *Productive* Speed is achieved when the right kind and amount of process architecture is put into place to stimulate rapid, but deep, decision cycles in management working sessions and ongoing performance checkpoints. Be sure to keep center stage the need to build speed through *simplicity* in the transformation constructs and *compression* in your corporate transformation game plan, Roadmap, and events. Again, speed achieved through careless omission of an important step or design element will have the opposite effect on transformation success.

Taking time to engage in meaningful dialogue with your team can also seem like a luxury that your limited schedule won't allow. However, leaders eventually discover that shortcutting dialogue to get to faster action only leads to confusion in execution, where debates are repeatedly revisited, problems are dealt with too late, and, hence, big decisions that could create profound breakthroughs are avoided. Leaders who have mastered the ability to drop in the zone with their teams and get deeply into issues quickly have discovered new levels of clarity, focus, and speed in taking decisive action, which, in turn, gets them to bigger breakthrough results faster.

Now let's return to the other essential elements in the structure of an accelerated transformation.

WHAT'S A "NO-SLACK" LAUNCH?

How can you effectively collapse the whole launch process into a short period of time in a meaningful and impactful way, while gaining not only precious time but also essential energy, commitment, and momentum? The "No-Slack Launch," which runs in parallel to the routine management process for a few months, reliably performs this task.[3]

First, lay out for the Senior Leadership Team, (SLT), next for the Extended Leadership Team, ELT, and then for all employees, a compressed Roadmap with specific waypoints and dates that everyone will step through on the way to refinement of your new business. Let everyone know what's up and when they will come aboard.

The Roadmap needs to be tightly scoped to the essentials of decisions, actions, and outcomes, not an endless list of work activities on a Gantt chart. With proper preparation and good design, you will be able to take your team and the teams reporting directly to them from confronting reality to finalization of the core transformation constructs and initiatives in three to four meetings, interspersed with pre-work and appropriate interim testing and refinements. The Roadmap needs to be a compressed one. Keep in mind that every time a team receives a few more weeks to complete one of the steps, they wait until the last week or so at best to bear down. By the time several extensions have been authorized, a three- to four-month, No-Slack Launch will have ballooned to six months, even a year or more.

Intensive involvement in the No-Slack Launch should place key executives outside their formal positions on the management team. For example, during the Launch sequence, they should be asked to serve as Co-Champions in the development of key initiatives and later to provide company-wide Execution "oversight" on the progress of their assigned initiative. These cross-organizational duties are performed in addition to being responsible as line executives for the achievement in their own department of *all* initiatives.

Pausing up front to make this kind of investment in a well-designed, tightly compressed structure of the ACT planning steps, each with all team members aboard and under the lights together, greatly accelerates the experience each member goes through to engage, explore, influence, and align to the new transformation agenda. The Transformation Leader needs to look for as many opportunities as possible for dialogue among the team members and to structure the leadership forums so that the airtime of dominant players is balanced against that available to more thoughtful and less vociferous team members. More about this in the next chapter.

This accelerated cycle is at the heart of becoming a strategically agile business that is positioned to disrupt markets rather than be trumped by unexpected and disruptive competitive attacks.

ROADMAP: THE BACKBONE OF TRANSFORMATION

The best way to avoid procrastination during the early Launch steps is to develop a compressed transformation *Roadmap* up front that lays out the important waypoints where there will be analysis, input, decisions, plans, and then execution. This architecture must include all the critical transformation principles of confronting reality, focus, alignment, engagement, and follow-through. In addition, it must clearly articulate when and where each person in the organization will have a chance to learn, provide input, and then make decisions and commitments that impact his or her area of responsibility. The No-Slack Launch at the front of this Roadmap that is embedded in the ACT process is shown in Exhibit 4.1.

Typically, you should compress the first three steps into no more than a three- to four-month timeframe, leaving only two to four weeks between major checkpoint sessions. If more time is allowed into the planning process up front, it will begin to weaken the Launch by undermining the sense of urgency, and it won't add quality and delays the process of learning.

Launch Speed = Simplicity x Compression

The *speed* that runs through all successful transformations is not the kind that should instill concern or fear. It is not the kind of speed that is achieved by oversimplification or purposefully or inadvertently skipping steps and activities that are on the transformation critical path. But recall, it is on the other side of complexity, where ACT resides. It is the kind of speed that is based on *simplicity* and *compression*. Speed is made up of many small things such as simplifying the transformation constructs and templates, minimizing the steps, tightly designing key events and decision processes that take place within them, and cleanly operationalizing and communicating the transformation initiatives.

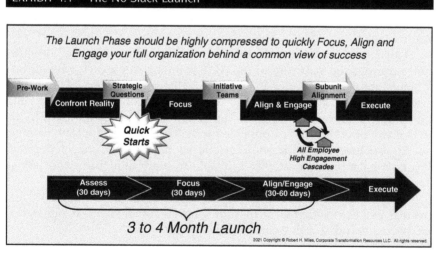

EXHIBIT 4.1   The No-Slack Launch

One good illustration of the latter is the set of standard templates that all leaders working on the Transformation Initiatives must continue to refine throughout the Launch Phase. This simple, sparse, consistent slide set for each Transformation Initiative is important to be presented at every venue from the early leadership team meeting all the way down through the Cascade rollout so that all employees can easily grasp their meaning and translate them for relevance and into personal commitments at their level. As Exhibit 4.2 reveals, each Transformation Initiative can and needs to be distilled to the set of a dozen or so slides. Parsimony is the key to an effective Transformation Initiative. Each slide is critical, first, for communicating and getting feedback for refinement, and later essential for rolling out to the whole organization in the cascading process.

Hold firm to this slide set, even to its consistent layout when you get requests from Initiative Co-Champions to deviate from this specific format or to tag other considerations to their main presentation deck format. It is far easier for the audience to compare and digest consistently presented information than for them to have to wade through unnecessary complexity. If some Co-Champions persist, on a case-by-case basis allow them to distribute supplemental material at the end of their module, but not as part of their presentation.

EXHIBIT 4.2   Template Set for Transformation Initiatives

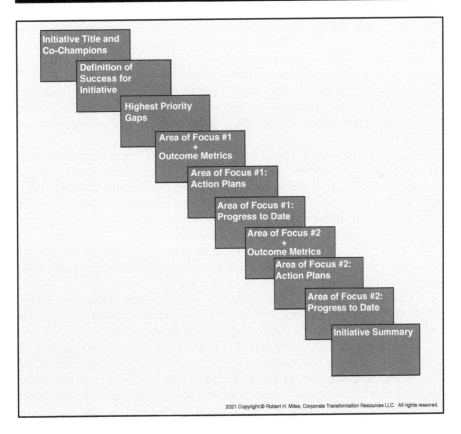

2021 Copyright © Robert H. Miles, Corporate Transformation Resources LLC. All rights reserved.

Reflecting on the chorus that speed through simplicity and compression is essential in transformation work, the CEO of an ACT-based high-tech transformation concluded,

> *I've had very few opportunities other than with this process when we've gotten everybody from the CEO all the way through the last person in the organization involved in hearing the same message, aligning goals, and making commitments in such a short time. I think a lot of people completely underestimate the power of getting the entire organization hearing the same simple message and behind a single focus from top to bottom. It was really amazing how much energy was created at one time.*

THE IN-BETWEEN WORK

One of the major causes of delay in launch efforts is the time allotted for getting work done between the meetings. We've all been to brainstorming meetings that generated long lists of ideas. But it usually takes a week to get the meeting notes published (if they ever come out). In the absence of tablework based on structured dialogue, a team of administrative support people usually labor for hours to translate scrawling from numerous flip-chart sheets into readable meeting notes. Leaders struggling to push on typically have to review the long lists of random, incomplete, and un-prioritized ideas before breaking them into categories and assigning them to interim work teams. A clumsy step like this between meetings typically adds at least another week or so of phone calls and lots of prodding and cajoling to get people to open up their schedules to take on the session's follow-on work. Project leaders then have to schedule the first meeting to talk about scope and purpose for their working team. Consequently, another two to three weeks can elapse before the first work session can get scheduled.

At this point, you are four to five weeks out from a Launch meeting, and nothing has happened to advance the thinking and planning. And it will take several more weeks to get the analysis done and the team report prepared for presentation and discussion at the next Launch meeting. By then, you've consumed two months between Launch meetings. Given that you need five scheduled Launch meetings with your SLTs and ELTs, you are into a minimum eight- to nine-month Launch Phase before anyone below the top three levels of leadership can become fully engaged in your transformation!

How can you effectively collapse the whole Launch process into three to four months? Without losing anything? In fact, while gaining not only pre-cious time but also energy, commitment, and momentum?

First, announce the complete timeline with prescheduled dates at the onset of the Launch. That way, everyone knows exactly what needs to be done in terms of decision points during the key working sessions and the analytical work that needs to take place between each main event. This en-ables your team to envision the full path, much like the speed skier. It will also send a strong signal of your commitment to stay the course for at least 15–16 months in the typical ACT-based transformation Roadmap.

Second, schedule the timing to either avoid or, if necessary, encompass other major corporate events so that you don't swamp people's calendars. If the latter, make sure that the transformation planning portion of your agenda does not receive short shrift.

Devil in the Meeting Details

There must be discipline to the work of executive leaders for a successful, rapid transformation Launch. Each of the five key Launch meetings of your team must be planned and structured in advance. What advance preparation needs to be done? What is the timed agenda for each convening of the leadership team? Who is presenting what? What specific questions will the tablework teams have to respond to? What worksheets will be developed to guide their deliberations and focus their report outs? What will be the likely next steps leading to the next meeting of the group during Launch? If you get the design right, the meeting will run itself, leaving you as Transformation Leader the luxury to listen more carefully, better time your inputs, and orchestrate smooth transitions from one difficult decision to the next. (Refer to Appendix 2, "ELT1 Meeting Notebook Skeleton," for a glimpse of how the agenda is laid out for these core SLT and ELT Meetings.)

Next, make sure to end each SLT and ELT Launch meeting with a 30- to 60-minute work session to kick off the first meeting of any teams that have been tasked to complete interim work before the next leadership meeting.

All these details must be planned well in advance. And to what effect?

When debriefed before closing even the first SLT meeting in an ACT-based Launch Phase, executives always report the meeting "broke all company records," and they say that "all company meetings should work like that." Their buy-in to your transformation starts right there with SLT Meeting #1.

So, make sure that your team knows well in advance when Launch meetings start and end and hold them to the full agenda. Establish a no-cut rule for the leadership team and ban early departures for flights. By not allowing the normal amount of slack to enter the system, you not only speed the cycle time to engage the full organization and shorten the time to generate results but also engineer a significant shift in the operating rhythm and meeting culture of the company. There will be more of a sense of the value of speed generated through real-time feedback and dialogue, tight frameworks to prioritize discussions and actions, and expedited (or eliminated) administrative tasks.

If you don't take charge of the first meeting in your transformation Launch, others certainly will fill the vacuum.

TRANSFORMATION INITIATIVE CO-CHAMPION STRUCTURE

Another somewhat different aspect of the ACT approach is that the core Transformation Initiatives are developed and initially launched by *Co-Champions* drawn from the SLT. They are announced by the CEO the moment the SLT has coalesced around the three to four corporate-wide Transformation

Initiatives, but before they become operationalized into Areas of Focus and Metrics.

Typically, it is said that if more than one person is in charge, then no one is in charge. But in this case, it is different. There are several compelling reasons to go with Co-Champions in rising to a corporate transformation challenge. First, it is too easy to ascribe initiatives focused on the market and customers to only the Marketing vice president. Similarly, talent or people engagement initiatives are often given just to the Human Resources vice president to run as some special new program. That leads to business-as-usual programs being launched by functional groups that the operations and field groups might or might not participate in or help drive. While that traditional authority structure may suffice under status quo conditions, it creates neither the robust corporate initiatives nor the company-wide traction during Execution needed for fundamental transformation.

So, the ACT-based approach calls for Co-Champions to operationalize each Transformation Initiative during Launch and to continue to provide "oversight" on progress during the Execute Phase. In fact, it recommends that all members of the SLT be a Co-Champion of one of the initiatives. If not, experience reveals that those not so involved from the onset will not fully understand and be engaged with the corporate Transformation Initiatives. Any SLT members who are given a hall pass during critical transformation meetings will cast very long shadows over their part of the enterprise during the Cascade and throughout the Execute Phase.

Let's consider two very different ways in which a talent Transformation Initiative may be implemented throughout a field organization.

In one example, the corporate transformation game plan has as one of its Transformation Initiatives a talent component, in which field executives opt to rely completely on the Human Resources function to do the work for them. Field executives periodically review and approve programs that Human Resources design. However, it becomes tough for the Human Resources teams to get the time for the reviews, much less create time in the field operations to get their programs implemented. Managers in the field fail to view talent management as a part of their "real" job and don't spend much time on it. The new hiring practices come off as just one more administrative policy guideline. The development program becomes viewed as an optional course to which field employees are sent only when they have slack time to work on courses for which their part of the organization had little say in the way of design. These poor implementation results may be traced back directly to the lack of accountability and ownership shouldered by line managers to develop and support the talent initiative. Such "siloed" organizations do not view collaboration as essential for success.

Contrast this situation with one in which business and functional departments each have their own commitments to support a corporate Transformation Initiative.

Marketing produces more effective campaigns when Sales provides input on how customers will respond. Engineering designs better products when Marketing provides customer and competitive analysis to guide the design process. Human Resources is more effective when local line managers actively participate in recruiting top talent. And, Manufacturing has higher quality when partnering early with Engineering so that products are designed to be easy to build from the start. The Co-Champion design initially helps to ensure that the typical gaps due to silos are bridged in the process of operationalizing each company-wide Transformation Initiative and later encourages each business and functional organization to contribute whatever they can to its achievement in an accelerated manner.

The best choices for Co-Champions of company-wide Transformation Initiatives are drawn from the SLT in a manner that results in pairings of functional staff executives with their counterparts in business units, operations, or field groups. These pairs of SLT Co-Champions are responsible for taking the lead on operationalizing their assigned initiative, vetting it in various SLT and ELT meetings along the Launch Phase Roadmap, and presenting it in a compelling and consistent (structured) manner for easy employee understanding and commitment/goal setting as part of the Cascade. Later, these Co-Champions are joined by Division Champions to form company-wide Execution "oversight" teams as the process moves beyond the Cascade to the Execute Phase. More about this in Chapter 9.

The typical ACT-based Initiative Co-Champion structure is shown in Exhibit 4.3. This structure is put in place by the CEO shortly after the transformation Roadmap is laid out, and it stays in place throughout the corporate transformation effort, which may involve several years. But during the compressed Launch Phase, the basic components of this structure consist of five major roles.

At the top, of course, is the Transformation Leader; in enterprise-level transformations, the CEO. His or her role as leader of the corporate transformation is quite straightforward. This is not something that can be delegated. This is an absolute. It is the CEO's role to lay out the transformation

EXHIBIT 4.3   Leading Transformation: Initiative Team Structure

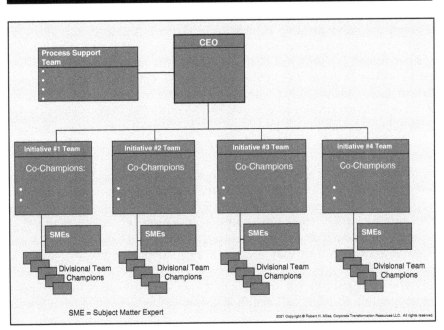

Roadmap, to create and enforce the "safe passage" environment so essential for high-quality dialogue and decision making, and to guide the leadership team to a corporate transformation game plan that is ready to put into Execution. The CEO must champion the unique ACT-based Cascade process. He or she must also rigorously follow through on performance execution. And the CEO must model the company values through his or her visible behaviors and decisions throughout the transformation journey.

Co-Champions drawn from the SLT come next. Their initial job is to adopt a cross-functional perspective on their assigned Transformation Initiative and operationalize it through several compressed rounds of vetting with their peers (SLTs) and with the subunit leadership teams (ELTs) reporting directly to them. Together, the SLT Co-Champions serve with the CEO as the *transformation steering committee*. And in this role, the no-cut policy applies. Like the CEO, they share the responsibility of leading the transformation and its Cascade in their own division in an aligned manner and modeling the values through their personal behaviors.

As the transformation crosses over from Launch to Execution, the company-wide initiative Co-Champions will be joined by Divisional Champions to form company-wide initiative teams that have Execution "oversight" responsibility. They monitor and report on progress with their company-wide Transformation Initiative and capture and disseminate leading practices on their initiative across the organization on a quarterly basis during the Execute Phase.

ALL-IMPORTANT PROCESS SUPPORT TEAM

The CEO and the senior executives serving as Initiative Co-Champions are supported by the Transformation Process Support Team, which enacts the staff- and consultant-support side of a leader-led ACT transformation. This all-important team consists of the ACT Process Architect and the Chief Administrative or Human Resources Officer, as Co-Chairs, supported by representatives, typically the heads of each of the major process disciplines; that is, leaders in the areas of Human Resources, Training and Development, Performance Management and Compensation, Strategic Planning, Communications, Employee Surveys, and so forth. This team reports directly to the CEO throughout all phases of the ACT-based corporate transformation. Its influence on the transforming organization is illustrated in Exhibit 4.4.

It is from the Process Support Team's "cat bird's seat" that the team's co-champions guide the alignment of the company's process disciplines in support of the transformation game plan. Here is where the detailed design and logistics for key transformation events spring, as well as where light facilitation of some of the key quarterly checkpoint events and Cascade rollout meetings comes; but always in the support role in a leader-led transformation.

The principal process architect is the ACT-based coach to the CEO or Transformation Leader and the SLT members, as well as to the Process Support Team. The Architect is usually from outside the organization and brings a wealth of experience and know-how to the Process Support Team. It

EXHIBIT 4.4   Roles of Transformation Support Team & Extended Teams

Process Support Team
- Provide Transformation support to the CEO, the Senior Leadership Team, and the Extended Leadership Team
- Support the design and facilitation of Transformation leadership events, checkpoints and cascades
- Align critical process/content areas to the Transformation:
  - Performance Management and Compensation
  - Employee Communications
  - Training, Development and Employee Surveys
  - Strategic Planning and Budgeting
- Oversee the roll out of the rapid, all-employee, high-engagement cascade and of the quarterly mini-cascades
- Serve as on-going liaisons to the Initiative Teams

Initiative Champions and Teams
- Lead the planning, cascade and execution oversight for the Initiative
- Maintain a cross-functional perspective on the Initiative
- Monitor performance of the Initiative
- Capture and disseminate leading practices on the Initiative
- Prepare presentation on Initiative for each quarterly ELT checkpoint meeting
- Provide quarterly content to support mini-cascades and communications campaign

Extended Leadership Team (CEO and Division Leadership Teams)
- Implement their Division's high-engagement cascade
- Lead Transformation in aligned manner in own Division
- Model the desired behaviors in their Division
- Actively support the on-going Communications Campaign.

is the Process Architect's job to ensure that the process disciplines in the organization have the insights, tools, and templates to enable them to support the transformation effort in an aligned manner as it moves through the various phases.

Often it is the case that the staff departments must hold in abeyance projects that are not aligned with the transformation game plan, or that might otherwise overload and gridlock the organization. It can be quite difficult for some support staff leaders to accept give-ups on projects that have been in their department's que for a long time and for which they had to work hard to get funded. But in an ACT-based transformation, they will find themselves on the front bumper of the effort, the first to align and commit to get behind the new Transformation Initiatives and required behavioral change expectations. The important leadership and internal support roles are summarized in Exhibit 4.4.

It is the role of the senior staff officer occupying the Support Team's other Co-Champion spot to ensure that the functional process discipline leaders provide their support in a timely manner that is aligned with the ACT-based transformation framework. It is also the responsibility of the senior process co-champion to ensure that the various process function leaders quickly learn to work together in an aligned manner to support the CEO or Transformation Leader and the SLT, and continue to do so on a just-in-time basis as the transformation moves from each phase to the next.

To repeat with emphasis, during an ACT-based transformation, leaders, line managers, and supervisors are in charge of the transformation in all levels of the organization, and they are the ones on front stage in important events and meetings of the transformation game plan.

In the spirit of the preplanning associated with all aspects of an ACT-based transformation, the work of the Process Support Team is tied to the transformation Roadmap, only always one step ahead. In fact, the team's required work products are so predictable its meetings and agendas are scheduled and published up front through the Launch Phase, as shown in Exhibit 4.5. This helps ensure that all Process Support Teams members are available when most needed.

EXHIBIT 4.5   Process Support Team Meeting Schedule: Launch Phase

Pre-scheduled Meetings During the Launch Phase		
Date	**Time**	**Agenda**
Th, 2/17	9:30-11:30	• Get acquainted • Orientation to ACT methodology and application to (organization) • Review of Transformation Progress • Update on Initiative Teams
Fri, 2/25	8:00-10:00	• Process disciplines: Review & Alignment discussions • Liaison assignments
Wed, 3/9	9:30-11:30	• SLT_2 Debriefing • Overview of All-EE, high-engagement cascade • ELT_1 Agenda, Planning and Logistics • Process disciplines alignment planning • Updates from Initiative Teams
Th, 3/17	9:30-11:30	• Final ELT_1 Planning & Logistics • Process disciplines alignment planning • Updates from Initiative Teams
Wed, 3/23	2:00-6:00	• ELT_1 Leader Prep Meeting Set up
Th, 3/24	7:30-5:30	• ELT_1 Leadership Meeting
Wed, 3/30	9:30-11:30	• Debrief ELT_1 • Initiative Cascade Planning • Process disciplines alignment planning • Feedback to Initiative Teams
Fri, 4/8	10:00-12:00	• Cascade Planning • Planning Performance Management Alignment with CTAs • Process disciplines alignment planning • Updates from Initiative Teams • EE Survey Plan Review
Th, 4/19	9:30-11:30	• Debrief SLT_3 • Prepare support for CEO and SLT Setting of CTAs • Finalize alignment of CTAs and Performance Management • Cascade Planning • Process disciplines alignment planning • Updates from Initiative Teams
Date	**Time**	**Agenda**
Th, 4/26	9:30-11:30	• Finalize Cascade Plan • Process disciplines alignment planning • Review of Executive CTA process and refine • Finalize EE Survey Plan • Updates from Initiative Teams
Th, 5/4	9:30-11:30	• Final Planning for ELT_2 Cascade • Finalize Kickoff: Agenda Notebook and Logistics • Updates from Initiative Teams
M, 5/10	2:00-6:00	• ELT_2 Cascade Kickoff Meeting Set Up
Tue, 5/11	7:30-5:30	• ELT_2 Leadership Cascade Kickoff Meeting
M, 5/16	9:30-11:30	• Debrief ELT_2 • Final EE Cascade Planning
TBD	TBD	• All-EE Cascade Launch

Finally, during the Launch Phase, the Co-Champions often invite *subject matter experts (SMEs)*, who are content and program management specialists, to help them operationalize their initiative. A member of the Process Support Team is designated as an on-going *liaison* to each Initiative Team to provide general support, ensure alignment among all the templates, and provide timely update to the Process Support Team on the progress on all initiatives.

Yes, this is a simple structure for such a huge undertaking. A light saddle for a racehorse comes to mind. That's what is meant by a *leader-led corporate transformation.*

"QUICK STARTS"

To put top spin on your transformation Launch, nothing builds early momentum and a sense of urgency like clear progress and early wins.

Just three weeks or so into an ACT-based transformation of a high-flying semiconductor chip company, which had lost its shine, the new CEO gathered his senior team for their first Confronting Reality meeting. They met to review market realities, customer opinions, and the results of confidential interviews with the key leaders of the company. All of those fact sets indicated that there were big problems to fix to get the company back into a high-growth mode.

To distill the most important focus areas, the group worked on an exercise to quickly identify the "really bold ideas" for moving the company forward and the "really stupid things to be avoided." That simple exercise netted out some urgent issues that had long been avoided but that deserved immediate attention. They ranged from the need to launch a new generation of products and reorganizing into profit and loss-oriented divisions to fixing morale and associated high talent turnover.

During a break in the session, the new CEO pulled a small circle of advisors together to contemplate the short lists of dos and don'ts the table-work teams had developed. After the larger group reconvened, most of the executives were expecting him to make some supportive comments about the quality of dialogue and thinking he observed during the previous session before introducing the next work session. In the back of their minds was the multiweek Launch Roadmap they had seen in his initial explanation of the process. This led them to expect that the process would take that long to unfold before real decisions would be made to cause action to take place. Not the case for this new CEO.

Instead, the new CEO opened the session by stating that the company appeared to have put itself in a position of being a generation and a half behind on technology. This would require potentially 18 months to two years to rectify. He went on to say that over the next couple of months, many tough decisions about current R&D spending would require more analysis and refinement of the strategy. On the subject of the morale issue, the CEO explained that the leadership team would work through a process over some period of time, first setting values and then living them and gradually restoring confidence in winning throughout the company. Making people feel better on the inside, on the other hand, he reasoned was something that every individual would need to address on his or her own. Raising morale would not be a focus of the transformation effort but would certainly be an expected outcome.

Finally, the new CEO addressed the organization design issues, agreeing with the team that the current design was not allowing leaders to make important decisions about their businesses. As a start-up, the original functional design had worked fine. As a growing public company, however, this structure had become too centrally focused and needed to be changed. He felt that if not addressed right off the bat, the antiquated structure would stifle progress on the transformation itself and the initiatives that would follow. So, he targeted restructuring as a *Quick Start*. In his mind, there was no need to have more dialogue or analysis about this obstacle, and no reason to wait for the full process to unfold before he acted. At that moment, he decided to change the structure and immediately tasked the vice president of Human Resources with initiating the design of the new divisional organization to be implemented immediately.

This decisive action, or Quick Start, sent a clear signal to the team that issues they brought up would be seriously considered for immediate action if warranted; that even the streamlined Launch process would be interrupted and accelerated for cause. It signaled to the team that this was not some overly bureaucratic process that was being followed. When the time was right to make a call and move on, there would be no waiting.

After being established by the executive leader, the Quick Start convention kept members of the leadership team on the edge of their seats for the remainder of their four-month Launch Phase. As a result, the team moved into the next steps in the ACT-based Launch with an acute sense that what they were working on would absolutely have an impact. As the CEO reflected, sometime following this intervention,

> *"'Quick Starts' established confidence in the organization that we could win. They were very powerful, and that sent a signal to the team that this was going to be an action-oriented process."*

One of the most difficult balances for a leader to strike is wanting to get out of the blocks fast versus taking the "time" up front to have deeper dialogue and engage a broader group to enrich the thinking and propagate ownership of the decisions. As you refine the architecture of your transformation process and get the effort launched, look for those major no-brainer issues that are getting in the way of progress, the ones that are aligned with the major Initiatives your teams are developing and don't require a lot more analysis to address. Take a few of them immediately as Quick Starts. People will appreciate your decisiveness and honesty, knowing that their time won't be wasted on a process that might not address the really important issues facing the company. The boost in energy and momentum you will experience will be palpable.

TIPS FOR STRUCTURING YOUR TRANSFORMATION LAUNCH

- Be parsimonious in adding extra nice-to-have steps and methods to the core ACT Roadmap, which is streamlined to enable and to avoid complexity and energy-sapping task overload.

- Opt for a No-Slack Launch that runs parallel to the routine management process so that the development of your transformation game plan does not receive short shrift.
- Lay out a transformation Roadmap that lets everyone know when and how they will become involved.
- Tilt your process toward motion, not analysis, to build early support and energy.
- Compress your Launch Phase into a three- to four-month timeline.
- Remember that *Productive Speed* in transformation comes from simplicity of content and compression of process, not from careless omissions or skipping essential steps.
- Carefully advance plan not only major transformation events but also the in-between work.
- Avoid having "wallflowers" on the SLT; they will cast large shadows over their part of the organization during the Cascade and Execute Phases.
- Make all SLT members a Co-Champion of a corporate Transformation Initiative during both launch planning and execution "oversight".
- Create a Transformation Process Support Team to make sure all the enterprise's process disciplines are aligned in support of the corporate transformation game plan.
- Launch "Quick Starts" before you complete the overall transformation game plan.
- Bias all phases of your transformation game plan to be leader-led at all levels, which is professional staff and consultant supported.

Notes

1. Portions of this chapter were adapted in part from Robert H. Miles and Michael Kanazawa, Big Ideas to Big Results: Leading Corporate Transformations in a Disruptive World. Second Edition, Pearson, 2016; and Robert H. Miles, Leading Corporate Transformation: A Blueprint for Business Renewal. Jossey-Bass Publishers, a division of John Wiley & Sons, 1997.

2. For more about organizational "imprinting," refer Robert H. Miles, Macro Organizational Behavior. Goodyear and Scott Foresman, 1980, pp. 251–253.

3. Robert H. Miles, "Accelerating Corporate Transformations – Don't Lose Your Nerve!" Harvard Business Review, January–February 2010.

CHAPTER 5

Crafting Your Launch Process

Rapid transformations are not achieved by structure alone; they also require a simple, robust, engaging process that is tailored to this big task.

Easily overlooked by strategic thinkers, but once unleashed in an organization, is a micro intervention that can profoundly affect the whole of the enterprise and its unfolding transformation.[1] It has everything to do with the way the organization is led through the transformation process at all levels. And if done well, it will speed and greatly increase the quality of your launch and it will positively impact the culture of the entire enterprise.

From the onset of transformation planning by the Senior Leadership Team (SLT) right down through the Cascade sessions in which individual contributors are brought aboard, this micro intervention is deployed to break down problem-solving and decision-making biases and intensively engage all concerned. It is embedded so deeply in the way Accelerated Corporate Transformation (ACT) clients work together that they come to absorb it into the way they lead the transformation and, ultimately, how they manage on a day-to-day basis. The same micro intervention becomes the centerpiece in the way Transformation Leaders setup and run the downstream Cascade meetings to engage and enlist all employees.

The intervention has three, robust, mutually reinforcing aspects, which are referred to in an ACT-based transformation project as *creating safe passage*, *structured dialogue*, and simply *tablework*. Each is easy to understand. They require only the instructions in this manual. Together, they are powerful enough, along with the ACT structural elements, especially the ACT Roadmap, to enable you to develop, launch, and sustain a rapid transformation. Better yet, if you start with them in the kickoff meeting of your Senior Leadership Team (SLT) and stick with them throughout your transformation roadmap, you will experience a palpable upgrade in management skills and culture throughout the enterprise, even before the halfway point in your first year of transformation.

DOI: 10.4324/9781003272724-5

Also, this chapter highlights two important perspectives – the internal and external – that figure heavily in the up front, Confronting Reality prework before transformation launch. It provides useful tools for capturing both realities.

CREATING SAFE PASSAGE FOR CONFRONTING REALITY

By *creating safe passage,* we mean that to begin developing a corporate transformation game plan and get the most of his or her SLT, the leader needs to set some ground rules and tee up relevant objective internal and external information, to govern how the team works together to confront reality, explore alternatives, and make decisions. The steps required are highlighted in Exhibit 5.1.

ACT uses *structured dialogue* and *tablework* in all important SLT meetings, starting with the initial Confronting Reality session (SLT1) that kicks off a corporate transformation launch. Such teams are made up of very different individuals; some with lots of power and influence, others with comparatively little.

Some hold sway over the most important businesses in the enterprise, while others are trying to get unproven ones off the ground. Some have a surfeit of resources, while others are scratching and angling for every dime. Some have been on the team forever, and others are newcomers from inside or outside the organization. Some majored in finance, others in engineering, others in marketing, others in operations and IT, others in people, and still others in hard knocks.

EXHIBIT 5.1   Creating "Safe Passage"

Step 1   **Lay out a clear roadmap from current to future state:**
- specific key events and deliverables
- show how and when people at different levels will become engaged

Step 2   **Agree on a simple set of ground rules to govern:**
- working together
- discussing new ideas
- engaging in critical thinking
- decision making

Step 3   **Have an objective third party collect difficult information:**
- what is working/what is not
- visions about new business and organization models
- data from customers and non-customers
- fact-based insights from outside the organization

Step 4   **Confront reality:**
- convene a well-designed event to facilitate structured dialogue and decision making among your executive leaders
- road test important aspects of your new model down below in the organization

Suffice it to say, if you assemble such a diverse team around a board-room table and conduct a discussion headed toward consequential decisions involving major reallocations of resources like it's a jump ball at a Final Four basketball tournament, you're not likely to get much in the way of a thoughtful outcome. Indeed, half of the assembled team probably won't actively participate. And most certainly, only the "winners" of the discussion and debate will be committed to the decision they wrested from their peers.

But we are getting ahead of ourselves. In short, as a Transformational Leader, you need to strive to make it safe for everyone to enter critical decision-making, structure their dialogue for success and create settings that reinforce these perspectives in all transformation planning activities.

Let's look at a few common pathologies in organizations that inhibit not just rapid transformation but management in general.

PATHOLOGIES TO UNDERSTAND

Denial is the opium of losers. Nothing guarantees fatal errors faster than seeing only what you want to see. Winning is all about realism, accepting the truth, and acting on it quickly and more effectively than your competitors. Seeing things from the market, customer, and community perspectives, from the front lines, and from the outside-in, that's what matters. History is littered with the defeats of deniers.

Denial takes many forms; one situation illustrates it well. A multibillion-dollar company had just assigned a newly appointed CEO and COO team from outside the firm. The primary charge from the Board was to reverse a five-year slide in sales.

Two weeks into the assignment to develop the process architecture for helping the company speed its transformation and strategy execution process, a small team had been given an office on the executive floor to conduct their work. The office had all the appearances of having been hastily vacated. There were still files in the drawers and a large map on the wall, with pins placed on once promised but long-forgotten projects. While cleaning out the files, the team noticed a document right on the top of a stack in one of the drawers. Titled "Strategic Options," the file was authored by one of the world's leading strategy consulting firms. It was dated two years prior to the team's arrival, and although aspects of the game had changed, it was still worth a look as part of the up-front discovery process.

Flipping past the first few pages, the team stopped at a sheet titled "Executive Summary Recommendations." There in front of them, with some items circled in red, were all in plain view the straight-up, harsh realities that needed to be addressed with urgency; only the report had been written and submitted to the previous CEO two years earlier.

The company's new executive leaders welcomed the team with hopeful comments about the ability to tee up the "real issues" that for so long had been taboo. The prior CEO clearly had access to the report and presumably had reviewed its recommendations. He just hadn't acted on any of them. In contrast, the new CEO and COO were very motivated to confront the realities surrounding the business they had inherited and were quick to put these data on the agenda for executive discussion. This recurrent story of strategies stored as binders on shelves or files in drawers is all too common and a clear reminder that many of the issues and recommended solutions are typically right there in plain sight but have simply not been confronted and implemented.

Taboo Topics

It is critical for leaders to set a tone that allows the team to confront reality. Even at the executive levels, certain taboo topics become routinely avoided, despite an abundance of pent-up energy to let out the truth. This is a unique window of opportunity that especially new incoming leaders cannot afford to keep closed.

It often takes just a bit of structured dialogue (the creation of a safe place to speak openly) and the guidance from the leader for a team to begin speaking plainly about the real roadblocks to progress. It is a fool's game to try to suppress the real issues. Everyone knows the problems exist whether they speak openly about them or not. People whisper in the halls or joke over drinks after work about them. But until the safe passage is provided, many people will not risk mentioning anything about them in front of the boss or aggressive peers. If it is not clear how the issues will be accepted or if anything will be done about them, the risk for speaking up with no clear benefit is high.

Sometimes, in the absence of structure and guidelines, more than simple dialogue and executive encouragement is needed to suspend taboo status. It often takes a little shock to the system to unlock the conversation, which can come from any level of management. At the worst-performing division of a global industrial products business, the team had spent a day and a half denying that they had any problems. Then, one exasperated and the brave manager came back from a lunch break and broke the logjam by playing over the sound system the country song, "Pissin' in the Wind." His colleagues immediately realized that what they had been doing all morning amounted to about the same thing. This is not necessarily a best-practice recommendation, but sometimes one brave soul needs to step up and call the team out onto the ice. More often that will need to be you as Transformation Leader.

Encouraging conversations that are critical of the company and leadership to be handled out in the open allows problems to be addressed sooner and new ideas to surface. To suppress these conversations does not make the issues go away; it just drives people into a quiet mode of resentment and cynicism. None of those behaviors are useful when looking to constructively confront reality. The willingness and ability of leaders to take constructive criticism is the starting point. But what kind of decision-making is best suited for transformational change planning?

DIALOGUE VERSUS DISCUSSION

Over two thousand years ago, Plato got it right when he observed that truth emerges only through dialogue. Socrates soon followed with a general appeal for more time spent through discourse or conversation to get to the bottom of human affairs.

There can be no real understanding, commitment, or, ultimately, engagement in the absence of dialogue. That is why *structured dialogue* needs to be a core element in leading a transformation or executing a bold, new strategy.

A critical distinction in conversations that most of us are typically unconscious of is the difference between *dialogue* and *discussion*. They are quite different modes of conversation. At the core, the purpose of having a dialogue is to search for deeper meaning and understanding. The essence of discussion is to net out differing opinions to get to a final answer. Both are necessary at different times and situations.

The Latin roots of the word *discussion* come from the same place as the words *percussion* or *concussion* and have to do with opposing views being batted back and forth. You know you are in the mode of discussion when, in the midst of a full meeting, two people begin to lock into a rapid back-and-forth with a lot of bystanders to their banter. Discussion is occurring when people are jockeying for airtime, working to have the winning idea, advocating positions, or arguing key points and assumptions. If someone else is speaking and you are trying to break in by saying, "Yes, but right, but just think about, let me make a point," then you are in discussion mode. Even if you are not speaking up but your mind is conjuring a rebuttal while the other person is still talking, you are in discussion mode.

Typically, businesspeople will naturally be in discussion mode most of the time. Most have been trained well to debate points, make convincing arguments, and influence others when a decision is due. Discussions are useful in getting to an answer or making a final decision. But discussions are not necessarily useful in generating a deep understanding of reality or generating innovative ideas for growth which are essentials at the beginning of a transformation.

Dialogue, on the other hand, as a form of conversation more focused on working toward a deeper understanding and discovering new possibilities. It is more about asking the right questions, not coming up with the right answers. Dialogue is often marked by short periods of silence while people are thinking through and internally integrating what has been said. There is no fight for airtime. You are more likely to hear questions such as, "Tell me what you mean by that," or "If we went with that, how would that change things?" As you listen to someone talking, if you are working to internalize what they are saying and integrate it into your thinking and mindset and building on or adding to their ideas, you are likely in a mode of dialogue.

To be clear, dialogue is not about "feel good" conversations, but rather is a tool for getting at tough truths about the business. A partner in a private equity firm described the value of dialogue well:

> *The dialogue is where the answers come from. People don't necessarily answer (due diligence) questions correctly in the beginning, but through the dialogue we collectively arrive at the right answers. Getting to the right allocations and profit models doesn't come from looking at spreadsheets but by really thinking about how the business actually operates. Once the right numbers are brought together and match reality, management easily comes to the same logical conclusions, and they make the decisions.*

When done correctly, dialogues end up as very powerful work sessions because they are carefully structured to facilitate everyone's initial input, make it safe to engage in courageous conversations that, more often than not, generate breakthrough ideas.

Generating Dialogue as a Leader

Sometimes even when leaders feel they have a real knack for open conversations with their teams, they still overpower others with their presence and style. For example, one CEO had a penchant for engaging in debate. The debate was his way of getting his team to engage in a topic, to explore different perspectives, and to finally come up with a quality decision. He was quite strong at debating and had more experience at a higher level than anybody else in the room; plus, he was competitive. So, he could usually win a debate. Not surprising, when he was looking to establish an open dialogue with his team, the result was that few, if any, people were willing to take him on. Controversial topics were avoided. There was no true confrontation of reality. The CEO left those forums wishing that more people had joined in and argued more vigorously. He really wanted more of their active participation.

When you are the leader, your answers, especially if provided too early, have a strong tendency to be the right ones at least for that moment. You will win every debate and dominate every discussion. But by knowing when to step back rely on a simple process to let your team dialogue to get at the truth, you will unlock a powerful transformation tool that is essential to confronting reality, which is imperative in the case of launching a transformation.

Canary in a Coal Mine

A year into the transformation launch at a large high-tech semiconductor manufacturer, a team of middle managers was convened to evaluate how the effort was going. The team was given several weeks to deliberate and tasked to deliver what its members thought were the biggest obstacles at one of the quarterly leadership meetings.

Most of the executives other than the new CEO were refugees from the company's failed old guard. It was the perception among middle managers that many of these company leaders were attempting to solve current corporate challenges the old way, with reactive restructurings, crisis management, and top-down decision-making. They believed many senior executives were not making difficult decisions and sticking with them. Therefore, heading the list of major obstacles to transformation was the very thorny issue of lack of trust and credibility of top management.

When their work was completed, the major challenge to the team had just begun: how to constructively confront their SLT with their major findings concerning the first year of their company's transformation effort and then to work with them to find solutions that could be put into action?

The members of the team felt quite responsible for their task. As one explained, "We now have 400 middle managers who are committed to the change process, and we're afraid of losing momentum."

The ground had been softened by having the senior executives get prepared to receive some hard feedback. The night before the middle manager presentation, the executives explored what was at stake with this intervention, how difficult it might be for their subordinates to speak candidly about the problems on their watch, how to avoid defensive responses to tough feedback, and what next steps they should be prepared to take in doing something constructive about what they learned.

The next morning, the tension was broken by the leader of the middle manager team, when he began the presentation by saying,

> *I feel like a canary going in to test the safety of a mine! (Audience laughter.) If my wings are still flapping after a few minutes, the folks with the real messages will come forward to present their parts of the middle manager feedback.*
>
> *The members of this group strongly condemn and disown any action or threat made toward any employee for constructively speaking their mind. Should this have occurred, or occur in the future, we strongly urge that individual to go immediately to the Ombudsman. We value open and honest communication.*

When the presentation to the senior executives was completed, the assembled group of executives and managers worked together in teams to identify the five most critical obstacles to the company's transformation effort, and then five teams, each also a mixture of senior and middle managers, were formed, assigned an obstacle, and instructed to identify the most important action steps that needed to be taken to remove it. Throughout the process, the CEO created a safe setting for this important confrontation of reality, and he placed the recommendations of these joint teams on the critical path of the second year of the company's transformation effort.

It was by thoroughly thinking through these process steps that the executives were able to effectively confront the reality of the transformation they had been leading and make substantive and timely midcourse corrections. A year later, the company was featured in the *San Francisco Chronicle* as "Silicon Valley's *Comeback Company of the Year*."[2] (Exhibit 5.2).

The most important outcome of this critical step in confronting reality is providing a safe passage that enables a group of employees to rapidly work through data and come to grips with some sobering and simple truths. One of the many time-tested ways of giving lower-level employees the confidence and courage to come out of the shadows to constructively confronting reality is ensuring safe passage. This is as true for VPs reporting to the CEO as it is later in your transformation roadmap for individual contributors addressing their front-line supervisors. Constructing a simple framework for dialogue, which you'll see more about later in the chapter, is critical. The reason being, if the canary's wings stop flapping as the first brave soul raises concerns and is ignored or chastised, nobody else will follow him into the conversation.

How can you unlock the *internal* truths to start your transformation with a sharp sense of reality?

EXHIBIT 5.2   Silicon Valley Corporate Comeback of the Year

National's Headliner Year

Monday, April 19, 1993

★ ★ ★ San Francisco Chronicle

Comeback of the Year

NATIONAL SEMICONDUCTOR

The Santa Clara-based semiconductor company may not have broken the billion-dollar profit barrier like rival Intel, but it still pulled off the biggest turnaround of the year. After taking a $150.4 million loss in 1991, National recorded $99.2 million in profits last year, ranking 40th in return on equity. As National reorganized to get more payback from research and attack new markets, the value of its shares also rose nearly 40 percent.

INITIAL EXECUTIVE INTERVIEWS

One good way to make it safe for people to criticize the status quo is to start with a strictly confidential round of individual interviews with the Senior Leadership Team (SLT) and Extended Leadership Team (ELT), the SLTs' direct reports. These one-on-ones are conducted before the SLT1 Confronting Reality Meeting by the ACT Process Architect, who serves as an objective third party. Many leaders will say up-front things like, "On my team we all know each other really well; nobody is shy for sure, so we can just open things up with each other in the meeting. So, I'm not sure we'll learn anything new from the interviews." These perspectives are very common. Most of the time, the interviews reveal that overall the leaders are right about many of the key points. However, the common interview experience creates a feeling that the team owns the issues themselves. More important, most leaders are not perfectly well-rounded. Each has his or her own "flat sides," which often become visible to the interviewer. They also get to know the ACT consultant and have a unique opportunity to provide important perspectives to him or her.

The advantage of having the ACT Process Architect conduct these up-front interviews is that it enables the consultant to get into a relationship with the senior leadership, to understand individual differences in skills and perspectives, and to establish trust that is essential for their transformation work together, which this intervention inaugurates. On the consultant's side, this is strictly a professional–client relationship with each member of the SLT and ELT. The report content is made up of scrambled verbatim quotes from the interviewees; so, they are unattributed. Moreover, individual results are not shared, including most importantly, the CEO or Transformation Leader.

The verbatim quotes are organized along the major categories in the survey protocol, and they are segmented into SLT and ELT groups by the ACT Process Architect, who also presents the results at the SLT1 Confronting

Reality Meeting. Because the results are presented in a non-attributed manner, each SLT member can identify his or her own comments throughout the presentation, but also privately see how they stack up on major issues against those of the SLTs and ELTs as a whole. The result is a very powerful up-front engagement of some of the thorniest issues that must be addressed by the Transformation Leader and the SLT at the beginning of the planning and launching effort. This approach simultaneously enables leaders to get to know themselves better while making it safe for them to enter a more authentic dialogue about real issues, as they work their way down the transformation road and refine their game plan.

The Executive Interview Protocol (in Appendix 1) is distributed to executives prior to their scheduled interview. This gives them time to consider their responses beforehand and makes it possible to cover three substantive topics with a one-hour sitting: (1) gauging the magnitude of change that will be required by the transformation, (2) assessing what parts of the organization- of the "total system" – will require the most improvement – the "Gaps," and (3) evaluating the functioning of the SLT and what it needs from the CEO or Transformation Leader. (An explanation of the Total System Analysis is provided in Chapter 6.) The findings are factored into the early SLT1 Confronting Reality Meeting that helps focus the transformation game plan.

By the end of the SLT1, the top leaders have processed this information, as well as inputs on the transformation "inhibitors" in their organization. They have also received an orientation to the ACT Method and its accelerators, together with relevant internal and external analyses. Afterward, the impression should be rising that they are not in Kansas anymore! Henceforth, the real dialogue will become the norm in their transformation.

THE OUTSIDE-IN PERSPECTIVE

In addition to a thorough internal diagnosis, for a true confrontation of reality, you must see your situation through the eyes of competitors and customers and other important stakeholders. Their reality is a big part of yours.

The best way to generate an outside-in perspective is to, well, go outside. Get beyond having conversations within the internal team in the same old setting. One company's method was to hold executive strategic planning sessions away from the corporate headquarters in less-traveled cities around the country where they had a market presence. The idea was to spend some time together as an executive team while competitively shopping the competition and making unscheduled visits to their own stores as if they were customers. Such visceral experiences go well beyond what you can get from a PowerPoint presentation of an internally generated competitive analysis or a report by the third-party market research house. Those analyses are useful as well, but they lack the real-world impact of firsthand experience.

Another vivid example of outside-in took place in a steel company's effort to transform from a manual to a computerized rolling operation. One of its Transformation Leader's first steps was to move the computer staff from their comfy downtown headquarters to a space inside the mill alongside the heavy, clamorous rolling operation, with only a long window separating the two operations. That really got their attention!

And still another example in the same vein is something I observed while writing this chapter. It involved "humanizing" the launch of Space X International's first manned re-useable Dragon Spaceship, based on a public–private partnership, which if successful will be truly transformative in many dimensions for the US space program. To elevate the focus and engagement of all this program's ground-based scientists and engineers, the Space X Chief Operations Officer had pictures of the two Dragon astronauts placed on all program employees' work orders on launch day.[3]

Send Employees Out

One of the more creative ways of confronting reality during an ACT project occurred in a large, highly unionized US utility, which launched a transformation while annually making $1 billion in net profits. The prospect of being able to actually pull off a major transformation of a company initially doing so well and hemmed in by overlays of complacent managers and union work rules was extremely challenging.

A creative mid-level executive was given the task of jump-starting the transformation. The biggest challenge he inherited was finding a way to get people motivated to get engaged in the process. His initial instincts were on the mark. He had to get managers and employees at all levels to understand the need for transformation and to leave their comfort zones. They would need to not only support, but actively lead the effort in their areas of responsibility. He first had to get everyone – managers, union leaders, and employees – to confront reality.

The competitive landscape confronting this large, staid utility was becoming occupied not by just the large, traditional rivals, with their heavy overheads and long investment horizons, but increasingly by agile new competitors. New independent power producers (IPPs) were beginning to cherry-pick the utility's highest-margin industrial customers. In addition, escalating deregulation of the electric utility industry was opening up the local market to all sorts of new competition from former regional monopolies and independent power brokers.

At one plant location, the urgency of the new reality had become clear to all. Employees at this location could climb to the top of the cooling tower, look out toward the horizon, and see the facilities of two large industrial customers that had been lost to new competitors. But for the majority of employees, the need for transformation was not as clear.

The executive's gut told him that the best way to serve up the new reality would not be from the work of consultants or staffers. Instead, he commissioned diagonal-slice teams, made up of executives, managers, union officials, and rank-and-file employees, to go out and engage with the new business realities. These diverse benchmarking teams researched, toured, and analyzed the operations of several large, rival power generation operations. They scrutinized the capabilities of the new IPPs. Indeed, many of the team members were initially puzzled by the fact that the new rivals would open their doors and books to them. During one of the first visits to one of these new, independent rivals, they asked why the company would be so open to a conversation with a competitor and were astonished by the response they got from its executive leader. He replied,

> *You guys are like a big aircraft carrier, and I'm a PT boat. You're too big and too cumbersome. You've got too much bureaucracy to turn that thing around as quickly as you need to turn it around. There's a new war that we're fighting, so I'm not concerned about you being a competitor.*

The arrogance that IPP executives thought they could beat [our] proud old company "in its own backyard" was convincing evidence for the bench-marking teams that significant change was not only needed, but essential. As our mid-level executive recalled,

> *What they saw blew their socks off because they discovered a totally different approach to the power generation business. They found the IPP plants well built, efficiently run, and, most important, focused on providing low-cost energy. The competitive spirit, employee empower-ment, cost focus, lean staffing, and work culture of these new competitors convinced the teams that fundamental, not the usual incremental change was required at their company.*

To complete the confronting reality phase, the executive had the teams de-velop their own reports and present them directly to the electric power generation employees, thereby completing the team members' ownership of the new reality while disseminating it in a credible way to everyone else.

Within two years, the utility had successfully completed the first leg of its transformation. Its managers, supervisors, and first-line employees were be-coming comfortable with their new vision state, it had eliminated hundreds of millions of dollars in overhead, and it had hammered out a "new deal" with its unions to support a more flexible and cost-effective work system.[4]

Talk with Customers and Noncustomers

Seeking the opinions of customers as well as noncustomers is another im-portant way to constructively confront reality. At one high-tech company, there seemed to be no shortage of issues being raised as the new CEO ar-rived. It was crisis mode, and there were lots of opinions on what was wrong. The sales team, in particular, had significant complaints about the product team's slow pace of new product development. In their view, that was the reason they had lost one of the company's largest customers, which, in turn, had driven the tailspin in revenue. The sales team claimed to be the voice of the customer and expected that view to be given heavy weight in the reality top management took into consideration when making key decisions.

The sales team argued that salespeople are on the front line with cus-tomers every day. "We know our customers very well, and they let us know what they need. Nobody in headquarters has that view of reality." Although in general, it is true that salespeople are closest to customers in terms of interaction, they also are likely to get a distorted view on what the customers really need. The nature of the sales–client relationship will tend to lead to discussions about features and price; not necessarily other areas such as the quality and integrity of the salespeople themselves, major new product line ideas, and supply-chain challenges. Sensing that the issue wasn't as simple as that of recent delays in product launches, the CEO embarked on a global tour to meet the company's customers himself.

Salespeople around the world geared up by preparing presentations for the CEO to make to their customers and setting up briefing meetings with them for the CEO. However, the CEO quickly put a stop to that activity and let the sales team know that the purpose of the conversations was not to pitch, but to listen. One of the first visits was to a large customer they had just lost. The CEO went in with no PowerPoint deck and no hard agenda – only with an intent to find out what had gone wrong. The CEO had the sales relationship manager bring only a blank tablet to take notes. They definitely were uncomfortable in that role. By the time the meeting was over, they had heard about many issues, not the least of which were problems with the sales team's handling of some serious product quality issues. The executives at the customer company commented that they had never had an open-ended meeting like that with a vendor and were shocked that the CEO and his team just listened.

In addition to talking with all customers, the CEO and his sales reps also conducted interviews with noncustomers or companies who bought exclusively from competitors. Often, it is uncomfortable to go talk with customers with whom you have not been successful with your sales efforts. However, they are quite often great sources of reality for you. They have nothing to lose by making suggestions for improvements and nothing to gain other than helping another potential vendor keep the market competitive, which is in their best interest. In this case, the noncustomers had the same suggestions as those of the large customers they had lost.

With notepads full of shots of reality from customers and noncustomers, the CEO returned to the office prepared to net out what internal people thought, what different functional groups thought, what customers thought, and what noncustomers thought. Among all those points of view was reality.

By paying careful attention to keeping the right pace in the transformation launch and ensuring that it begins and continues with the outsideIn perspective in mind, leaders will be able to infuse their process with reality and keep enough tension between what could be possible and what they are currently doing to sustain the high levels of energy and focus essential for success. It is the challenge of balancing the inside and outside views that makes all the difference in the effectiveness of the confronting reality part of your launch prework.

HOW TABLEWORK AND STRUCTURED DIALOGUE WORK

So much for some useful ways to get the internal and external realities on the table for discussion. Now let us turn attention to the specific tools to deploy for facilitating dialogue and critical decision-making about them.

Following countless applications across different industries, organization types, and global cultures, an incredibly simple and seemingly mundane but very powerful vehicle for consistently generating high-quality dialogue has emerged. For simplicity, let's just call it *tablework*. Here's how tablework team exercises work.

First, most small and large, transformation meetings begin with a transfer of carefully crafted modules of information – a brief presentation from the front of the room at an event along with the transformation roadmap – before participants turn to their tables and dig in to make sense of it and hopefully translate it into a decision that will be put into action or referred for further study. By now you get the sense that in an ACT-guided environment, considerable preparation would have been devoted to making this presentation material as simple and compelling as possible. Having said that, the first rule after receiving the presentation, but before breaking into tablework is to allow only questions for clarification. Don't let anyone jump the gun with their first ideas or pet responses or fire volleys back and forth across the boardroom or hotel conference center before the presenter takes a seat.

Second, shortly after responding briefly to those, and only those qualifying questions, you must disaggregate the group before later reconvening them for presentation and decision-making in the general forum. Make sure to break the assembled group down into tablework teams.

If the group is relatively small, such as an assembly of the SLT, after the factual presentation, break the attendees into three- to four-person tablework teams that literally meet around the corners of the conference table. A larger group is broken down into smaller groups of no more than six to seven people seated at round tables assembled in a large room (e.g., a hotel ballroom). The reason for this number is that if you have more people per dialogue group, there will not be enough airtime for everyone to participate in a reasonable time frame. Please note that in both cases, no one leaves the room.

Tablework teams are not breakout teams, who have to depart the scene in search of remote places to meet and who waste precious time with their comings and goings. It was breakout teams that gave rise to the notion of "herding cats" because of all the lost time spent chasing around for participants when they had left the main forum. Not having to chase them because of the tablework option probably saves an hour more each meeting day.

Even for large gatherings of supervisors with their employees, it is recommended that you set up a large ballroom at a hotel, full of round tables, each buzzing in a structured dialogue on the same question.

Such very large gatherings can accommodate allpeople of the same organizational level, sorted into dozens of tablework teams at round tables with their supervisors, where their work together can be intimate, efficient, and engaging. The roar of conversations across such large settings is palpable. It makes tablework teams aware that all other teams at the gathering are working on the same problems, but from different perspectives. The third rule is to have very clear instructions and a simple output template to address each specific question. Exhibit 5.3 shows the typical instructions relying on structured dialogue for a tablework team.

Fourth, the time needs to be fixed and relatively constrained for each question to drive for clarity and the appropriate level of analysis and decision-making. Most tablework sessions take only about an hour each. Every tablework team that experiences successful dialogue always mentions that it would be nice to have had more time. But every workgroup that tries to leave the time open-ended only generates an overthinking of the issues and generates longer, unprioritized lists than are required.

EXHIBIT 5.3   Tablework Team Instructions

Tablework Team Instructions

Purpose:
- To help refine a major *Transformation Initiative* upon which we will intensely focus to accelerate the transformation of the company.

1. Each Tablework Team will have time to answer the assigned questions on the Worksheets that follow.

2. All members of the Tablework Team are expected to actively respond to the assigned questions, actively listen to the responses of other team members, prioritize importance of each response, and then help select the most important responses to each question.

3. Tablework Team process:

  a. Individuals take a moment to come up with their own answers to each question.

  b. Taking one question at a time, each member should share his or her most important response to the first question. Once *all* members have had an opportunity to nominate a response and have it recorded, anyone having a very different response should be offered the opportunity to add it to the list. Then, with the entire list of responses to the question in view, the **Facilitator** should help the team arrive at the *top* response(s) to the question, and the **Recorder** should record them on the team's Worksheet.

  c. The processin (b) above should be repeated for the other questions.

  d. The team **Presenter** should be prepared to present in the open forum the team's Worksheet.

  e. The team **Reporter** should turn in both Worksheets at the conclusion of the session.

Dialogue by its nature is intended to create expansive conversations about a topic, so if you start without a tight structure of scope, timing, and specific answer formats, the conversation will drift all over the place and generate no useful conclusions. So, keep it focused and time-bound.

Tablework Teams and Roles

With clear instructions in hand, tablework starts with each person taking a few minutes to quietly consider his or her responses to the assigned question response. This quiet time at the beginning is essential. It allows the internal thinkers a chance to process the questions before the extroverts start generating active conversation. During this initial quiet time, each person jots down his or her answers on a worksheet.

This simple, initial reflective task forces each group member to engage with the subject matter and arrive at preliminary ideas before the conversation starts. This helps clarify people's thoughts before the active dialogue begins. It helps to avoid rambling speeches and encourages everyone not just the most vocal to become more emboldened to share answers that might appear to be too controversial or unrealistic before the real dialogue begins in earnest.

Next, during tablework, each person is invited to share his or her best answer or two with the team. At this point, again, it is important to follow first with only questions for clarification from others. This is a time to get ideas out in the open, not to edit or judge them. It allows people of lower organizational standing or less forceful personalities to be fully heard. Oftentimes, the best new ideas come from unexpected people.

To make sure that the tablework team follows this routine, three roles are assigned before the process begins. One of the tablework participants serves as a *Recorder*, who is responsible for capturing all the ideas and ultimately prioritizing them on a structured worksheet (see the standard ACT worksheet for Tablework teams in Exhibit 5.4). This structure also keeps tablework "bullies" from shutting down other points of view before they are fully shared, typically with comments like, "You know, in the field it really isn't like that" or "Technically, you're right, but it will never work because." In addition, a *Facilitator* and a *Presenter* are identified by the team members. The appointed Facilitator leads the discussion at the table to select the best answers to share with the larger meeting group and keeps the process on track and on time. When the task is completed, the Recorder notes the final answers on a worksheet, and the Presenter, who has been organizing his or her thoughts during the group's deliberations, will stand up and share the opinions and recommendations that have been summarized on the team's worksheet.

Each tablework team will have generated dialogue and then prioritized, weeded, and captured the best ideas. Multiply that by every tablework team in the open transformation event forum. As readouts are done in the presence of the larger group, typically common threads emerge. It is easy to see where

---

EXHIBIT 5.4   Transformation Initiative Worksheet

Team #_____

1. Do you agree with the **Definition of Success** articulated for this Initiative? ____Yes ____No Please explain:	4. Do you agree with the **Outcome Metrics** that have been proposed for this Initiative? ____Yes ____No Please explain:
2. Are these the most important **Gaps** that have to be closed in order to achieve this Initiative? ____Yes ____No Please explain:	5. Are these the right **Commitments to Action** to drive this Initiative in the coming year? ____Yes ____No Please explain:
3. Do you agree with the **Areas of Focus** that have been selected for this Initiative? ____Yes ____No Please explain:	6. What are the **really bold things** we could do to drive this Initiative in the coming year that ought to be seriously considered?
	7. What are the **really stupid things** we need to avoid that would hurt our chances of achieving this Initiative? *Recorder:* Please turn in at end of session.

consensus exists and where there is disagreement; where inferences and assumptions are clear or specifically where they require further study. This structure of readouts also protects the individuals from any worry about putting forth controversial topics as they are reporting on the team's work, not just voicing their opinions. When a Transformation Leader is committed to structured dialogue, he or she reinforces safe passage and facilitates streamlined decision-making. Think of the power of this intervention when leaders at all levels receive and deploy this micro intervention throughout the organization during the cascade rollout.

What arguably is quite simplistic is also a powerful method for rapidly engaging an entire organization. An executive who has led both Business Sales and Human Resources departments in back-to-back appointments at a multibillion-dollar company underscored a critical aspect of the tablework process when he said to us,

> *Simplicity has to be a part of this. The agendas, meeting designs, and even the questions asked, need to be simple. This lets the people focus on doing the thinking rather than running through complex presentations or programs. The value is in the discussions with each other. And when it is simple enough, people all the way down to the front lines can use the same tools and meeting designs to lead their teams.*

The only remaining step in the tablework process is to close the loop on how leaders will accept the input from the group. This is an important step. Participants in a tablework dialogue will want to know that their feedback was heard and is being genuinely considered. There is a temptation for many leaders to process the feedback immediately and come to conclusions and answers on the spot. But that can undermine the idea that full consideration will be made of the ideas.

To close well, the process requires that the leader share his or her observations about the quality of the dialogue and the ideas that have been presented. The worksheets from each tablework group should be collected for further analysis. Note that there is no need to collect every individual's worksheet; that just creates an overload of items the team has already weeded out and defeats the purpose of providing "safe passage" of participants for some of their important but controversial ideas.

Notice also that nothing has been mentioned about the ubiquitous use of "flip charts," which often accompany group work. They are banished from the ACT Method's tablework in favor of simply structured team worksheets, which are used to channel consistent analyses and presentations and for study after the event. Occasionally, collaborative wisdom-of-the-crowd software solutions are used by tablework teams to input their answers and have them instantly captured and presented along with those of their fellow table groups. But save them for the larger events during the Cascade Phase.

The advantage of the software solutions is that those same ideas can be immediately ranked and rated for prioritization, with that information captured and presented back the open forum concludes. The caution is not to let digital equipment become distractions during the few, compressed but critical transformation events. Or even more to the point, digitalization can have a role in these transformation venues; but not at the expense of productive speed which derives from process simplicity and compression.

Finally, a commitment needs to be made by the leader that the feedback received will shape the thinking in the revised plans and commitments. Indeed, before the group breaks up, the leader should announce the future milestones in the process and when people can expect to hear the final outcomes. Other output from the meeting will require future study, and these assignments and delivery dates must be communicated before the event closes. This results in real work in real-time with concrete outcomes and next steps, which most meetings cannot promise. If you have already come to a full conclusion and don't want to change your mind on a particular topic, don't open a dialogue about it.

This and the preceding chapter have focused on what a Transformation Leader must set up before launch; the *Prework*. First is the need to establish and communicate to all involved from the get-go a transformation *roadmap*, to let everyone understand the scope of the transformation game plan and senior leadership's commitment to launching and sustaining it. Such a roadmap importantly lets everyone know how and when they will become involved in the process. Just publishing such a roadmap commits leaders to see its course through, which initially is laid out for a minimum of 15–18 months from the time the transformation gauntlet is laid down.

The roadmap must be complemented with a safe and reliable *process* for engaging first, the top three levels of leadership, and later, everyone in the enterprise.

As we have observed the first stop on the roadmap is Confronting Reality. It is crucial that the internal and external realities be boiled down in the prework for this kickoff event so it can be easily presented and reviewed in simple, bite-sized hunks, which lend themselves to structured dialogue and tablework.

Once the structured dialogue is routinely seeded into the transformation launch meetings, senior executives become accustomed to running meetings and making decisions in that manner. Then they take the structured dialogue to important meetings with their own leadership teams, and so on, until the tablework approach it entails becomes the way in which managers and employees at all levels engage with the transformation game plan and set their personal commitments to action to support it. It is the way the cascade to all managers and employees is conducted by immediate supervisors at each level and every department in the enterprise. As one division president of an oil and gas services company put it,

> *This process has shown me how to lead from the back of the room. And what is amazing is that by letting my team dialogue, they are coming up with their own tough decisions, and for the most part all I need to do is agree and help them with resources. That is so much easier and effective than driving it all myself.*

CONFRONTING REALITY KICKOFF WORKSHOP (SLT1)

One of the best ways to observe the structure and process design principles in action is in the first major event in an ACT-based transformation, the

Confronting Reality Kickoff Workshop, or SLT1. This workshop is conducted as soon as the transformation project *prework* has been completed. The external and internal perspectives have been distilled, as well as relevant competitor, market, and/or stakeholder analyses. The CEO or Transformation Leader has been able to absorb and reflect on this information, consult with relevant subject matter experts and confidants, and become comfortable with the ACT Method. Among these inputs are the results from the Readiness Survey, the Initial Executive Interviews, and the OutsideIn reports.

This is the first encounter of the SLT within the ACT-based transformation game plan and its operating principles, as shown in Exhibit 5.5. It is the first step in the Launch Roadmap. It is usually held in a Board Room and led by the CEO or Transformation Leader. In attendance are his or her direct reports as well as the ACT consultant and a couple of senior staff observers from the transformation Process Support Team.

Based on these inputs from the Prework, the Transformation Leader will have been able to formulate *preliminary* constructs that will eventually define the vision state that the transformation effort will seek, including such constructs as Purpose, Strategic Vision, Success Model, and so forth. The Process Support Team will have been oriented to their role in the ACT-based transformation and given a seat along with the ACT Consultant at the right hand of the Transformation Leader. From that perch, they will have begun to align their support functions to the transformation game plan and to work with the ACT consultant on planning and supporting the major transformation event (Exhibit 5.6).

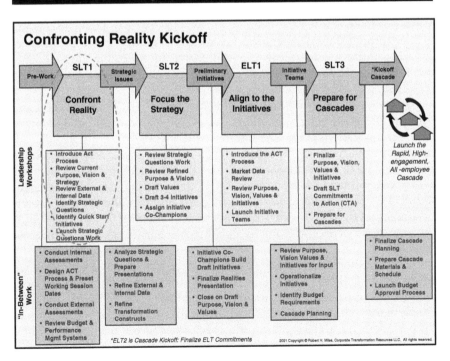

EXHIBIT 5.5   Confronting Reality Kickoff

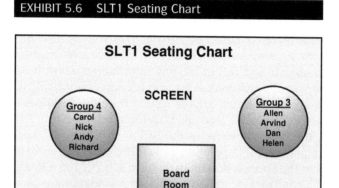

The module subjects are predictable. Except for the module overviewing the ACT framework, more time is allocated in each module for table work and structured dialogue with customized worksheets and report summary forms than for the presentation itself. Following the brief welcome (15 min) and followed by an overview of the ACT process and the roles SLTs will play leading it (30 min), the workshop settles into a predictable rhythm. The Transformation Leader summarizes the major external realities (30 min), SLTs break into tablework Teams and follow the structured dialogue routine (30 min), until team reports (major takeaways and open questions) are shared and then discussed in the open forum (30 min). After a brief break, the same sequence is repeated in a similarly compressed module by the ACT consultant regarding the confidential Transformation Readiness Survey and Initial Executive Interviews. A light lunch is served where participants sit (30 min).

After lunch, the modular rhythm resumes. First, the Transformation Leader presents the external realities, followed by tablework dialogue, report outs, and discussion. He or she follows with a similar module devoted to a preliminary overview of the major transformation constructs which define the vision state to which the intended journey is headed; drafts of things such as Purpose, Strategic Vision, Success Model, and so on. The last major module asks SLTs to step back from the day's work to identify any strategic questions that need to be answered, as well as identify any "Quick Starts" that may be tackled right away to signal strong early commitment and bias for action.

The Transformation Leader closes the session with thanks for a job well done, summarizes his or her major take-aways and to-dos coming out of the discussions, and makes assignments for the "in-between" work, including "Quick Starts" and open strategic and organizational issues required to advance to the SLT2 Meeting. Next, the Leader solicits a quick round robin on individual reactions to the day from the senior leaders. He or she closes by reaffirming the commitment to leading throughout the transformation roadmap during the Launch and Cascade Phases and through the first full year of execution and requests that the SLTs block out their calendars accordingly. Usually, a half-hour is set aside after the official agenda for assigned teams to take a moment to plan their interim work before leaving the venue. If not, it can easily take a week for team members to initiate their assignments.

In this initial senior leadership encounter, the distinctive structure and process aspects of an ACT-based transformation get seeded into an organization. If you get it right here, just think how easy it will be to roll your transformation out quickly and in an engaged and aligned manner, through the various levels of management to all your employees during the Cascade Phase.

The Confronting Reality Workshop is the first of three dedicated meetings of the Senior Leadership Team (SLT) in the Launch Phase of the transformation. The senior executives will be joined by their direct supports for two additional Launch meetings of the Extended Leadership Team (ELT), the last of which (ELT2) will kickoff the Cascade Phase. Depending on how much internal and external data has to be reviewed and synthesized, the SLT1 may have to take a day and a half to get through its multi-module agenda; but thereafter, all SLT and ELT Meetings, including quarterly checkpoints during the first year of the Execute Phase will require one day apiece. To accomplish the objectives of this ambitious agenda, much thought must be devoted to simplifying the key constructs and compressing the time over the target for each one of them, the core ACT-based principle of successful rapid transformations.

One more perspective on this transformation leadership approach:

Top strategy development is handled primarily by the senior executives, in most cases the SLT and ELT; but it should be opened for dialogue with the middle management team for a reality check and input. So, when you design your timeline for engaging the organization in during a transformation, be sure to build in this appropriate but always compressed cycle for dialogue before the final decisions are made. The tablework method, when coupled with structured dialogue and safe passage, gets everyone's ideas out on the table before requiring everyone to narrow the choices down to those that can have the greatest potential for impact. It quickly puts the power in the hands of leaders at every level in the organization to engage their direct team in dialogue, idea generation, decision-making, and ultimately, commitment setting.

In many conventional management approaches, lower-level leaders are only expected to play passive roles: they are simply asked to be the conduit of messages and expectations from above and make the changes they are told to implement in their workgroups. Passive participation, such as simply allowing or enabling changes, results in a compliance culture that is relegated to the status quo or incremental improvement aspirations. But by establishing the ACT process guidelines, you propagate a very active approach to engagement in dialogue and decision-making at the SLT and ELT levels that soon thereafter is cascaded down through the entire organization. We will return to the critical Cascade Phase of a rapid, leader-led transformation in Chapter 8.

The rest of the book will pace you through the major Phases of the transformation game plan: *Focus, Align, Engage,* and *Execute.*

TIPS FOR CRAFTING YOUR TRANSFORMATION PROCESS:

- Make sure to start your transformation Launch Phase by *"creating safe passage;"* don't send any canaries into your coal mine!
- Incorporate *"structured dialogue"* and *"tablework"* into every event along with the transformation roadmap.
- Understand the difference between *"dialogue"* and *"discussion,"* and when and how to employ them.
- Deploy these ACT-based principles from your first transformation meeting with the Senior Leadership Team all the way down to every transformation meeting between supervisors and employees.
- And remember, dialogue and tablework actually speed your transformation, rather than slow down its progress.
- Enrich your Confronting Reality kickoff session with an internal perspective based on a round of confidential, third-party interviews with your next two levels of leaders.
- Creatively look at things from the external perspectives of customers, noncustomers, competitors, and other stakeholders.
- Get your employees outside to see firsthand what's really going on.

Notes

1. Portions of this chapter were adapted in part from Robert H. Miles and Michael Kanazawa, Big Ideas to Big Results: Leading Corporate Transformations in a Disruptive World. Second Edition, Pearson, 2016; and Robert H. Miles, Leading Corporate Transformation: A Blueprint for Business Renewal, Jossey-Bass Publishers, A Division of John Wiley & Sons, 1997.
2. The origins of the Accelerated Corporate Transformation (ACT) methodology are discussed in Robert H. Miles, Leading Corporate Transformation: A Blueprint for Business Renewal, San Francisco: Josey-Bass Publishers, a Division of John Wiley and Sons, 1997.
3. Dana Perino, Fox News Daily Briefing, May 27, 2020.
4. Robert H. Miles, "Type I Transformation: Repositioning America's Most Admired Utility," Leading Corporate Transformation: A Blueprint for Business Renewal. San Francisco: Jossey–Bass Publishers, a Division of John Wiley and Sons, 1997, pp. 83–126.

CHAPTER 6

The Focus Phase

Focus is not about doing more with less, but rather "Doing more ON less."

Successful transformation leaders must work with their executive team to distill out of the purpose, strategic vision, and success model developed in the Confronting Reality task a limited set of coordinated, enterprise-wide initiatives that form the tracks along which the transformation game plan will proceed. [1] The executive team, working together under mutually agreed-upon ground rules and a proven process architecture, must create the *Transformation Arrow*, a plan-on-a-page that contains the core transformation constructs to which all components and employees of the organization will align.

However, before outlining how best to do this, you need to understand why the transformation arrow is so important. Its main function is to enable the leadership team to articulate the new state to which the organization desires to move. One that delivers delight to customers, a better environment for employees, and greater value for shareholders and other stakeholders. To serve these objectives well and do so at the transformation pace and level of change, the team cannot simply serve up a new set of loosely assembled, uncoordinated initiatives that are pancaked on those already proliferating in the enterprise.

Let's briefly review the challenges of the Gridlock inhibitor to transformation before we lay out in detail its antidote.

GRIDLOCK AND THE TASK OVERLOAD EPIDEMIC

Even without having to rise to a transformation challenge, needless complexity exists in the main, not the exception in today's organizations. Much of what people are assigned to do could be left undone without damage to the bottom line. Managers and employees in many organizations are operating on extreme task overload. In reality, only a few critical initiatives they are pursuing have the potential for making a big difference. Most of the items on everyone's to-do list never get fully attended to anyway.

DOI: 10.4324/9781003272724-6

In the good name of tuning up core processes to drive efficiency, form has often overtaken function in many organizations. People scorecard everything that moves, launch multiple process-change initiatives in every business function, often simultaneously, and demand that everything be treated as a priority. Caught in the clutches of organizational attention deficit disorder, these enterprises need the simplicity of a well-conceived, well-orchestrated game plan, transformation, or otherwise.

Especially during a fundamental transformation, people and resources have to be more focused on the highest impact areas. Those *Areas of Focus* that can contribute the earliest results and the most to the shift in strategic direction must receive an immediate, unfairly generous share of the available resources. Yet, at the same time, employees need to keep a steady strain on all the other routine things that involve ongoing incremental improvements as part of their job performance.

Regardless of the coping method that emerges informally in a gridlocked organization, the message is clear. The need to focus – for simplicity and impact – is a tough idea to get across to a team of leaders, each of whom is trying to drive his or her own major programs. A common fear of many leaders is that if they admit that the organization is doing too much, they will lose their ability to motivate the team to do more. When such leaders keep piling on new initiatives, it becomes political suicide for a team member to throw up the white flag and call out the issue of task overload. Instead, everyone hunkers down further, scrambling for ways to check the boxes on their task lists as fast as they can.

The simple fact remains: You can launch as many initiatives as you want, but the capacity to execute will become a choke point in reaching results if your major initiatives are not sorted, prioritized, and sequenced. It takes a leader, seeing the pattern of gridlock and stepping up to prioritize initiatives and set a clear direction, to get started.

THE LEADER'S CHALLENGE: *"DOING MORE ON LESS"*

Focus is not about doing less work overall, but rather *"doing more ON less."* You need not give up on the call for transformational improvements in the organization and its businesses. You must be willing to shoulder the risks of clearly articulating a tight focus on what will and won't be done to get there. As transformation leader, you need to lead the way by making tough choices and less hedging of bets, then trust your team to execute with more accountability and impact now that you are calling on them to drive further against fewer goals.

One of the most damaging business catchphrases in recent history has been "doing more with less." This has become an excuse to pancake initiatives and reduce resources to support each of them; predictable outcomes when a leader lacks the fortitude to narrow the focus. What you need to demonstrate in your own choices and in what you expect of others is *"doing more ON less,"* focusing everyone on quantum improvement of the critical few activities that will provide the greatest impact. This is definitely true when it comes to selecting the few, major *initiatives* for your transformation.

SHARPENING THE TRANSFORMATION ARROW

Company leaders will often state up front that they already have a strategy. On the flip side, a survey of over 11,000 employees revealed that only 48% understand the organizational strategy and goals, and only 53% feel that they are focused on the organization's goals. Is it any wonder that leaders are frustrated that their transformation agendas are not being implemented?[2]

Strategies are often ambiguous, overly complex, and too lofty. They simply aren't taken to a granular enough level to be translated into simple, compelling transformation initiatives. Indeed, a majority of large ACT-based transformation projects begin immediately following the presentation of analyses and recommendations and then departure of strategic planning and market research boutiques, and after operational reports of internal fact-finding teams have been submitted. This is when the triage of all that input begins and then ends with the articulation of a limited number of simple but powerful transformation initiatives. This is the primary work of the ACT-assisted Senior Leadership Team and their direct reports (the Extended Leadership Team) during the Focus Phase.

One-Page View of the Future

When asked to create a short list of things learned from prior transformation experiences, the CEO of a $16 billion energy company noted that an often-overlooked element in successfully driving transformations is a "one-page" view of the desired future state. To illustrate the one-pager, he developed with his team a succinct summary of how the Purpose, Strategic vision, Business Strategy or Success Model, Values, Transformation Initiatives, and Commitments to Action all tied together in a cohesive, easy to communicate and recall, one-page summary. As the CEO reflected,

> It's memorable, easy to communicate, and easy to reference. If people can't remember the strategy, they can't act on it. And it is amazing how many times you need to communicate the same direction, over and over again to get it to stick. The one-pager does that. And the hard work and real value comes up front in getting the executive team to make the tough decisions that allow you to focus the business so tightly that it can fit on one page.

Another CEO of a large high-tech company based in Silicon Valley took the one-page concept and during the launch of a pivotal transformation and turned it into an arrow metaphor for his globally dispersed employees. Roughly he said, "We're going to sharpen our strategic arrow, and then we're going to put all of our wood behind it!" This is the origin the transformation arrow in the ACT-based transformation game plan Exhibit 6.1.

The Transformation Arrow

In the arrowhead reside the basic "what's" of the transformation. What we want to become and achieve because of our transformation effort. The usual suspects are the purpose, strategic vision, success model, and values. The

EXHIBIT 6.1   The Transformation Arrow

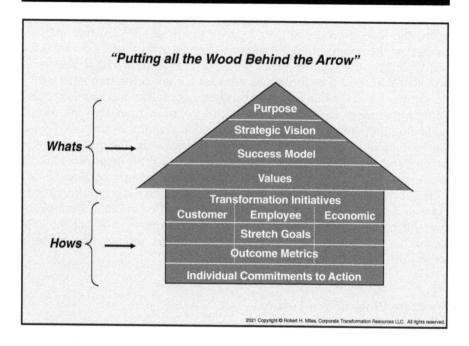

"how's" that reside in the shaft, consist of few major, carefully selected transformation initiatives and corresponding commitments to action, which are set at all organizational levels by all employees to tightly align performance and behaviors throughout the enterprise.

Begin work of the leadership team during the focus phase with the internal and external perspectives from their early confronting reality deliberations. Next, distill a purpose and strategic vision. Then conduct a total-system analysis of the company, comparing the current state versus the desired vision state. By the time the team has worked through these steps, the selection and refinement of the all-important transformation initiatives should be straightforward.

In this chapter, the core elements that reside in the top of the arrow will be introduced first. Next, the conduct of a total-system analysis will be described. The chapter will end with the derivation and structure of transformation initiatives. The values and commitment to action constructs will be saved for the next chapter on the Align Phase in the ACT Method.

THE "WHAT'S" OF A TRANSFORMATION GAME PLAN

Articulating a Purpose

Purpose in the transformation context relates to knowing why your company exists, what value it creates in the world, and how it contributes positively to others. For example, an iconic motorcycle company has a purpose to "fulfill dreams of personal freedom." A top performing airline lives by the purpose to "connect people to what is most important in their lives." In addition, an e-book platform company follows the purpose "to make available in less than 60 seconds every book, ever written, in any language." What is common in the purpose construct and in these examples is that they are statements about bringing value to others and are not defined by the assets or markets that the company competes in today.

As a result, the purpose serves as an ambition for the organization to continually strive to serve customers, employees, and partners better. This translates into a shared inspiration to innovate and disrupt outdated ways of competing. Purpose draws out an emotional quality that puts people in the role of delivering value to others, not just going to work to do a job. In fact, recent research indicates that over 90% of companies either have or are developing a purpose for their company. Further, 70% of leaders at these global companies believe it is important to integrate purpose into core business functions, with purpose including a balanced view of value for customers, benefit for greater society, and financial returns for shareholders. However, the same report indicates that only 37% say their success model and operations are well aligned with their purpose.[3]

Leveraged correctly, purpose becomes a focal point to align the essence and definition of the organization including the strategic vision, success model, and values. It is also a powerful driver in corporate transformations, which require high levels of engagement, motivation, and passion at all levels to succeed. A clear purpose also provides a basis for setting investment priorities and making business decisions. As an example, a retail pharmacy developed the purpose of "helping people on their path to better health" to motivate a transformation to a new type of blended retail and healthcare company. Using the purpose as a catalyst to reposition the company and reinvigorate the organization, leaders realized that selling cigarettes in their stores no longer fit with the purpose of the company. In a bold move, the company decided to stop selling cigarettes, which was approximately a $2 billion per year line of business. In the first quarter after making the bold move and sticking with their commitment to their purpose, revenue increased by more than 10%.

Developing a purpose for your company is not a trivial task. Although often communicated as an inspirational statement, purpose is a much more complex concept that embodies the reason for being, the essence of what is different, the journey and path the organization is on, and what value it brings to the world. Begin by considering how the enterprise started. What early imprinting did its founder leave? What did its products or services do for customers that they weren't getting elsewhere? Think about why customers, employees, and other stakeholders are better off today because of what the company does and what attracts them in a magnetic way to the organization beyond just the products and services. Purpose developed in this way becomes a north star to guide the strategic vision all the way through the entirety of the initiatives, operations, and culture shift in a corporate transformation.

Creating a Strategic Vision

Beyond purpose, a clear view of what success may look like on the horizon is important as well. However, one of the most commonly heard strategic visions in the business sector today is, "We want to be a market leader and to be an X billion-dollar player in our market." It's a statement about market position and financial results. Those are fine aspirations, but a strategy to be an X billion-dollar player does not work well as a complete vision for focusing and aligning execution. Focusing on an end outcome metric without a clear articulation about the critical requirements to reach the goal allows the leadership team to demand results without providing direction. That does not produce the kind of focused alignment and execution needed to generate the breakthrough results the leaders are hoping to achieve.[4]

A Strategic Vision should serve as more than just an aspiration to achieve a numerical goal. Instead, the following are guidelines to use in judging the quality of your vision statement. A vision statement should,

- State what employees will be doing or how markets will be responding when success is achieved.
- Clarify the general playing field (set boundary conditions).
- Specify which of the company's core competencies are unique.
- Signal an aspiration-driven level of achievement.

Some truly great strategic visions over time have never been achieved. Finite thinkers will say its heresy to set a vision that isn't achievable. But visionaries know that a great vision continuously stretches execution by creating a constant tension between current success and greater possibilities. In contrast, finite visions have finite endings.

For example, Nordstrom's company vision has remained unchanged for more than 100 years since its establishment in 1901: "Offer the customer the best possible service, selection, quality, and value." [5] This clearly places service first, which is still the hallmark of Nordstrom's business. In another example, Microsoft's original vision was to see "a computer on every desk and in every home, running Microsoft software."[6] This sounded like a pipe dream at one point, but has been almost fully realized today. Just imagine if Microsoft stopped by saying, "We want to be a billion-dollar player and a market-leading operating systems company in the world." That would have been a very limiting vision compared to where the company's growth has taken it.

But where, exactly, should a transformation leader focus a company? Often it is useful to begin an executive session with a simple, but telling, exercise. Sometimes all it takes to get visioning started is a simple, projective technique that involves members of the leadership team writing about what they believe their organization will have achieved or will look like in the future if the transformation they are planning is successful. One creative way to tee up a strategic visioning dialogue is to ask members of the leadership team to fashion a *Wall Street Journal* headliner about how successful the organization has become in three or five years, to be shared and discussed with their peers. Following a thorough confronting reality session, involving a sharing of timely internal and external data, such a relatively quick and straightforward exercise usually enables the assembled decision makers to immediately identify the key strategic vision elements, which can then be refined and vetted before being placed in the arrowhead. But keep in mind, the process of developing a purpose and strategic vision must be both creative and grounded in analysis. Projective techniques like the one discussed above stimulate the creative process, which then needs to be grounded in an understanding of customers, competitors, and what employees are passionate about and capable of doing.

With such simple interventions, the purpose and strategic vision can be generated without having to waste months of committee work and elaborate brainstorming sessions that cause this second major step in the transformation planning process to bog down.

To be effective, the strategic vision must be grounded in a rigorous success model, and, from that model, distilled into a few specific transformation initiatives, each of which is tied to bold, but unambiguous outcome measures. The success model succinctly summarizes how the organization will allocate resources, keep score, and ultimately achieve breakthrough results within the intent and scope of its unique purpose and particular strategic vision.

Distilling the Success Model

The old Albert Einstein saying goes something like this, *"The definition of insanity is continuing to do the same thing and expecting a different outcome."* Similarly, in the work of leading a transformation, you're not going to get very far along the path to a bold, new vision if you continue to allocate resources and measure progress the same ways you have done in the past. The essential vehicle for effectively reallocating your limited resources is to create a Success Model that is uniquely designed to test and support your new strategic vision. If developed for a company, this success model should also reveal how you will grow the earnings stream so that you can increasingly improve your ability to access debt and equity sources in order to accelerate progress of your transformation. Finally, such a model should also reveal what businesses or activities need to be eliminated or downsized to free resources to support the momentum to the vision state.

Keep in mind in constructing your initial success model, the techniques of incremental change and continuous process improvement are applicable for many situations, but if exclusively pursued to support a transformation challenge, they will only ensure an increased performance gap when compared to more agile competitors operating in a rapid transformation mode. In some cases when facing a transformation challenge the best you can initially do is create a broad strategic vision of what the desired future organizational state may look like, construct a success model to go with it, articulate an initially imprecise but comprehensive future state, identify a few major transformation initiatives to focus and channel the initial transformation effort, and develop a general roadmap that organizes the steps forward. As progress is made along the critical path of the transformation journey, the strategic vision, success model, future organizational state, and transformation initiatives can be refined.

The success model developed by a leadership team to fundamentally turn around their high-tech manufacturing company is illustrative. The CEO applied the following straightforward framework to develop their starting transformative success model:

> *Step 1: Take one of your key financial statements; the income statement or balance sheet, for example.*

> *Step 2: Benchmark each item on the statement: obtain market research data from your industry association and from your competitors as to what 's average, and what the best companies are achieving.*

> *Step 3: From the benchmark numbers, set difficult but achievable targets for your company.*

> *Step 4: When you have done this for each key business parameter, you will have produced a model defining what success means to your organization.*

Then, include the draft success model as a key element in your early confronting reality leadership event and later as a core part of the transformation game plan you cascade down for relevance and alignment for each element and level in the organization.

The high-tech team's initial success model, shown in Exhibit 6.2, was focused on the company's financials, which is typical in a turnaround transformation challenge. The model was updated as new performance achievements were logged and as the company's leaders learned more and more about what to expect as the transformation unfolded. Important income statement components are shown in the top half of the table, and key balance sheet metrics are depicted in the bottom half. During the first performance year, the primary focus was to be on growing gross profits, managing assets, and achieving and holding break-even expenses. For many of the company's engineering-oriented managers, these were new concepts, and much of the first year of the transformation execution phase was spent schooling them in these turnaround business basics.

By the end of the first two performance years, the CEO declared a transition to phase two on the company's transformation and the success model was revised as shown in Exhibit 6.3.

Another example of an initial success model of a global company facing another difficult but different transformation challenge in a very different industry is illustrated in Exhibit 6.4. It shows how the firm planned to allocate resources differently and where it would invest for competitive advantage. In this simple case, the success model supports a strategic vision of a company looking to differentiate itself based on staying ahead of competitors with technology and providing more value in customer service. More incremental funding will be devoted to technology (5%) and customer service (2%). To fund those differentiators, a focus on cost savings in the supply chain (5%) and leveraging channel partners (4%) will generate enough savings to net the company a 2% profitability advantage that can be used to go straight into earnings or to have additional pricing flexibility when needed compared with competitors.

This simple articulation of the company's success model makes clear to all employees what their part of the organization specifically needs to contribute. In this case, the technology division's primary focus was going to be on innovation and speed to market. In strategic supply, the primary focus would be on cost savings. In the marketing channels organization, creating large-scale partnerships would become critical; for customer service, the focus would be on high quality.

EXHIBIT 6.2   Success Model for Semiconductor Company's Turnaround

	Launch Year	FY1	FY2	FY3	FY4	FY5
Income Statement Metrics:						
Sales (M$)	1,686	1,820	2,048	2,287	2,546	2,836
Sales growth (% yr to yr)	-0.9%	7.9%	12.5%	11.7%	11.3%	11.4%
Gross profit margin (%)	27.4%	33.2%	35.8%	37.4%	37.2%	39.2%
Profit before taxes (M$) (incl. interest income)	24.4	129.1	201.7	265	312.1	398
Profitbefore taxes (%)	1.4%	7.1%	9.8%	11.6%	12.3%	14.0%
Net Earnings (M$)	(126.6)	109.7	161.3	185.5	218.5	262.7
Earnings per share ($)	(1.23)	0.88	1.31	1.53	1.86	2.28
Balance Sheet Metrics:						
Cash balance ($000s)	144	133	159	230	250	285
Total debt ($000s)	48	44	40	69	120	131
Equity ($000s)[1]	522	628	790	904	953	1,051
ROE[2]	(24.3%)	19.1%	22.8%	21.9%	23.5%	26.2%
RONA[2] (before taxes)	(28.7%)	25.6%	32.1%	36.0%	39.0%	45.3%

[1]Equity and net assets are both yearly averages
[2]Return is before preferred stock dividend

EXHIBIT 6.3   Business Success Models: Initial, Current and Future

Financial Metrics	Phase I		Transition to Phase II
	Initial 5-year Model	Current Actuals	
Gross profit	40%	42%	45%
Profit before taxes	13%	14%	17%
Net income	7%	9%	11%
Return on net assets	18%	38%	28%
Financial leverage	1.1	0.7	0.9
Return on equity	20%	27%	25%

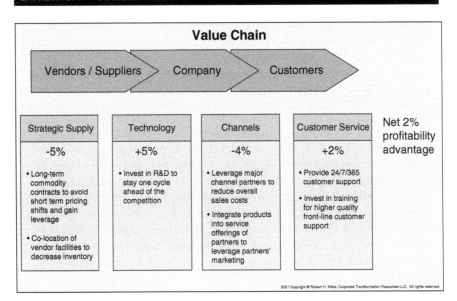

EXHIBIT 6.4   Success Model

Value Chain

Vendors / Suppliers → Company → Customers

Strategic Supply	Technology	Channels	Customer Service	Net 2% profitability advantage
-5%	+5%	-4%	+2%	
• Long-term commodity contracts to avoid short term pricing shifts and gain leverage • Co-location of vendor facilities to decrease inventory	• Invest in R&D to stay one cycle ahead of the competition	• Leverage major channel partners to reduce overall sales costs • Integrate products into service offerings of partners to leverage partners' marketing	• Provide 24/7/365 customer support • Invest in training for higher quality front-line customer support	

Due Diligence on Yourselves

A great example in the private sector of what can be done to figure out the best business success model quickly is the work of private equity investment firms. These firms buy companies using their own capital and debt, stay on as primary owners for several years while turning around or supercharging performance, and then sell the company at a gain.

The cycle time up front for assessing the true value of a company and determining how much to pay for it is very short. This is known as the due diligence period. During that time, a very small team from the private equity firm will dig into the details of the target company's financials, operations, sales channels, customer service, and other supporting organizations to see where real value is generated and determine where there might be pockets that are underleveraged. They also look for high-risk areas.

For corporations, the simple question is: "How does this business and industry really work, how does it create value, and what are the likely financial consequences of the model's success?" Often, the last step in business modeling is the development of a set of high-level pro forma financial statements that highlight the key success metrics. Sometimes in highly uncertain situations, the best you can do is lay out a set of alternative scenarios associated with performance consequences.

In this manner, private equity firms are able in a matter of days or a couple of weeks to come up with an accurate picture of the target business and the underlying drivers of value. How can they get to the answers for those questions so quickly? First, there is a short, relatively fixed time frame for them to make up their minds on a bid for a company. In the case of private equity, the deal will be lost to others if decisions can't be made quickly.

Would be transformation leaders often underestimate the speed possible in moving from planning to execution. Based on experience, it should only take a few weeks for a small group of people to develop an initial working strategic vision and success model to refine and vet during the focus and align phases of a transformation.

Why do so many executive teams never reach the same level of depth and specificity that private equity investors find in a matter of weeks? According to the managing principal in one of the large private equity firms,

> *There are a few common reasons we've found for management missing some of the drivers of value available to them. Often, people have not gone back and challenged cost allocations in the business, and the business has changed. As a result, they don't know where the real profitability is coming from. At times, people may have incentives to make a particular part of the business look better than it is. In addition, too much can be taken for granted in profit and cost expectations around the business based on high-level statements made by past executives and owners. People have a tendency to make things overly complex, and usually the real answers are pretty simple.*

There is no reason that transformation leaders cannot conduct rapid due diligence on themselves, an essential front-end step in a successful corporate transformation process. The following are some tips for doing this yourself in a business organization.

First, the analysis team needs to have a clear mandate and high-level support so that its members can raise and analyze all the tough questions that others have been afraid to ask. One good way to cover all the tough questions is to follow a due diligence checklist that is typically used in buyout situations to guide the work of the due diligence team. These lists include preset items that must be validated and include items such as the following:

Market
- Market size and growth of key business lines

Customers
- Customer loyalty and willingness to re-up contracts
- Value and quality of core products and technologies from external perspective
- Confirmation of differentiators from external sources

Competition
- Market share trends and competitive positioning
- Reasons for any recent competitive losses

Company
- Profitability by business unit
- Capabilities and loyalty of key employees

Leveraging this type of checklist ensures that the tough questions get addressed in the right depth, right up front. Not surprising, internal managers generally know where the skeletons are, and some may try to protect certain data from seeing the light of day. In addition, due diligence teams often conduct customer as well as noncustomer interviews to serve as a vital reality check to balance against the internal-only views of people, processes, and technologies. Finally, such due diligence teams will insist upon open access to and full candor with all members of the top executive team.

In the transformation effort of a large business firm, often the equivalent of an "internal due diligence team" will typically consist of some operational vice presidents or directors with financial analysts in support. Then, after the confronting reality session – where the transformation roadmap is kicked off and fueled with the facts from the due diligence – the full Senior Leadership Team (SLT) will engage in determining the biggest levers available for improving the business success model. Based on the experience and knowledge within the team, members are broken into smaller teams to take on a prioritized set of issues associated with the success model for the purpose of fully assessing them and developing recommendations. Within a matter of two weeks, the SLT regroups to collectively wrestle with the various recommendations to improve the success model before they conclude on the highest-impact changes that need to be made.

And not surprising, it is essential for the leadership team to have an experienced objective third party to guide them safely and surely through their due diligence on themselves.

According to our private equity executive,

> *Private equity investors are often much more willing to push things to the edge to find the performance limits of a business than existing owners, which is another reason private investors can find new value in old companies. They typically are more willing to encourage management to take the risk of testing traditional limits.*

Having operationalized key elements in the transformation arrowhead – the "what's" – it is time to turn to putting the wood – the "how's" – behind the arrow.

TOTAL SYSTEMS ANALYSIS

The next step in the transformation game plan is to identify the few important *Transformation Initiatives* along which the fundamental changes needed in the organization will unfold. The desired vision state must be translated into an organization design that uniquely supports it. This step requires a *total-system* template that combines and configures the formal and informal elements of the organization into a state of tight "fit" with the vision state being sought. It lays the groundwork for realigning the internal context of the organization to support the journey toward vision state, and it concludes with the identification and articulation of the major transformation initiatives.[7]

To be effective, a total-system analysis of the current organizational state and of the future state needed to uniquely support the strategic vision of a transformation effort must incorporate several considerations. First, the framework must comprise all the major categories of the organization design. Yet it must do so as parsimoniously as possible. Reliance on too few design elements or levers oversimplifies the task of implementing the vision through organization design. Inclusion of too many design elements burdens the analytical and implementation process and risks confusion from overlap and redundancy.

The total-system perspective reminds us that it is critical to make simultaneous changes across all dimensions of the organization during a transformation. For transformation success, a big change in one of these elements usually requires commensurate changes in all the other total-system elements. Moreover, the rapid pace required by transformations demands that people and organizational culture and competencies evolve into alignment with the direct, ACT-based intervention. Indeed, the cycle time of change needed to rise to a major transformation challenge these days has been reduced dramatically, making the ability to orchestrate simultaneous organizational adjustments a distinctive competitive advantage. As we say, the need for speed is now pervasive.

The total-system approach requires not only that all the elements of the organization be configured to uniquely support movement to the desired vision state, but also that they be closely aligned to reinforce each other. All the elements of the organization are interdependent in their effects on organizational performance and behavior. Again, be aware, big changes in one or a few of the elements of the organization without corresponding changes in the other element tend to create chaos, as important design elements begin to pull the organization in different directions. Therefore, when fundamental change is required, it is not advisable to proceed sequentially in the redesign of the organization. The challenge is to move boldly on all fronts simultaneously.

The total-system framework that has been developed from practice to support ACT-based transformations is shown in Exhibit 6.5.

The definitions for each element of the template are summarized in Exhibit 6.6.

EXHIBIT 6.5 Total-System Approach to Transformation Planning

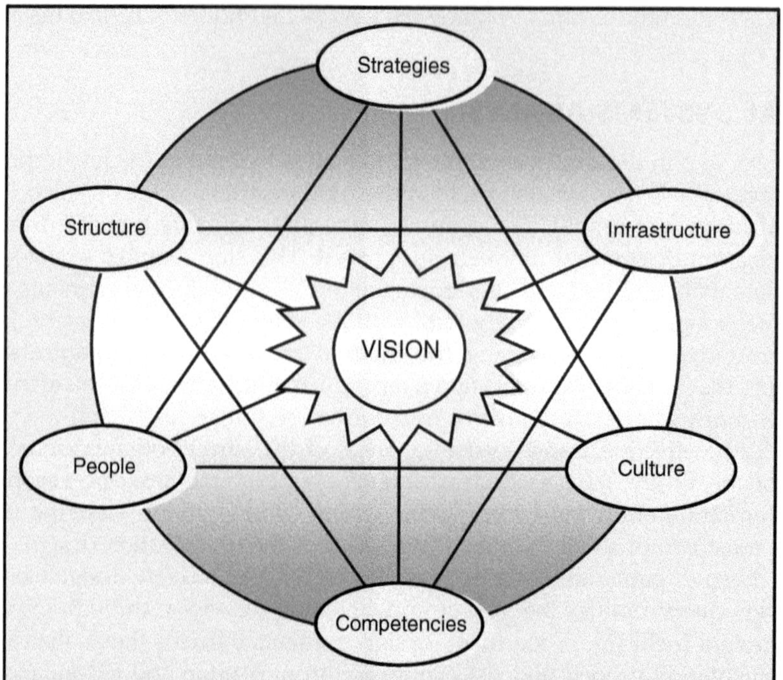

Source: Robert H. Miles, Leading Corporate Transformation, 1997, p. 35

EXHIBIT 6.6 Total-System Framework: Definitions

Organizational Design Element	Definitions
Vision	The purpose and mission of the organization and the supporting business success model
Strategies	The primary bases upon which an organization allocates resources to differentiate itself from competitors, create customer value, and achieve exemplary performance to realize its vision
Structure	The formal structural arrangements of the organization that delineate its basic units of authority and accountability and the "overlays" that regulate the interdependencies the formal arrangements create
Infrastructure	The formal systems and processes that reinforce the intentions of the organization's structure and strategies, including the basic measurement, control, planning, information, human resource, operations, communications, and resource allocation systems
People	The nature of the workforce, including work-experience, skills, needs, preferences, maturity level, perceptions, orientations, and diversity, as well as the view of the role of the workforce in the organization
Competencies	The core competencies of the organization as a whole; what an organization does particularly well
Culture	The values and beliefs that are shared by most of the people in an organization, and the style and behavior of its leaders; more a matter of what people and leaders do than what they say

The template is centered around the vision that is the object of a transformation effort. Surrounding the vision are the key formal and informal elements of organization design. Strategies, Structure, and Infrastructure, the formal design levers, are in general easier to diagnose and alter because they are more readily observed and measured. The informal design levers include People as well as organizational Culture (values and management style) and Competencies. These elements are more difficult to alter in a short period of time and are generally more elusive in diagnosis because of their subjectivity. (Recall that one of the ways to tee up the total-system analysis is through the initial executive interviews with the top three levels of leaders, as discussed in Chapter 5. Also, see the interview form in Appendix 1 at the rear of the book.)

In summary, the comprehensive but parsimonious total-system approach is an essential component in transformation planning. Without such a simple template and language system to underpin especially early executive-level dialogue and soon thereafter down through the ranks, orchestration of the elements of organization toward the desired vision state can become hopelessly disordered. Moreover, without such an approach there is little chance of preventing a proliferation of well-intended but uncoordinated change initiatives or improvement programs from overwhelming the total system and frustrating those who are trying to launch a transformation. Additionally, because of the interdependence of the elements of organization, the absence of a well-understood, widely accepted organizing framework can result in a situation in which major change initiatives cancel the effects of each other or even inadvertently push the organization in a direction different from that established by the transformation vision.

The Gaps

The primary purpose of a total-system analysis in the launch period of corporate transformation is to identify the major *"gaps"* on each design element, between the current and desired vision states. These gaps translate into creative tensions that help excite members of the organization to action, gauge the magnitude of the transformation required, and reveal the vector along which the vision journey must proceed.[8]

Gaps between the current and vision states must first be prioritized in terms of the magnitude of change required to close them. The highest priority – biggest – gaps must be sorted into a few major clusters of related gaps. From these clusters are drawn the initiatives that receive primary focus during the journey to the vision state. The funnel in Exhibit 6.8 illustrates the process for narrowing down a Purpose and Strategic Vision to a focused set of enterprise-wide transformation initiatives. The remainder of this chapter shows how to operationalize the Transformation Initiatives as shown in Exhibit 6.7.

TRANSFORMATION INITIATIVES: THE "HOW'S"

You've refined and vetted your purpose and strategic vision and developed and tested the supporting success model. It is time to complete the focusing and alignment steps in your transformation launch process. You must now clearly and carefully operationalize the most important part of the

EXHIBIT 6.7   The Gaps: Current versus Desired Vision States

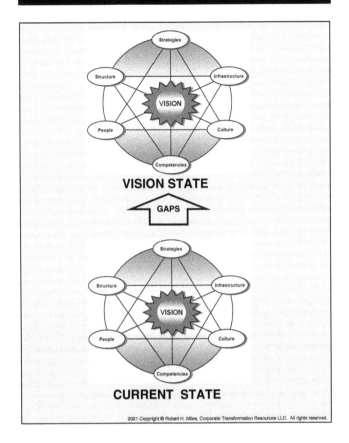

EXHIBIT 6.8   The Transformation Planning Funnel

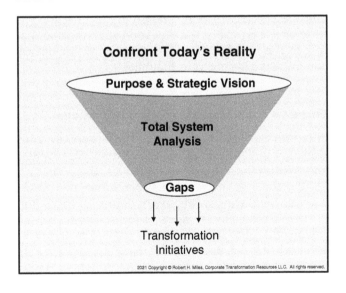

"how's" of the transformation game plan: the transformation initiatives, or TIs.

Let's take a closer look at this important element in your transformation game plan.

Transformation initiatives, or *TIs,* contain the major *areas of focus* in which quantum change is needed to successfully lead a transformation. It is critical to *focus* organizational resources and human energy for sustained periods of time to achieve rapid transformational change without confusing employees with too much complexity and saddling them with task overload. The visioning process and the total-system diagnosis have served as reliable tools for setting the stage for this needed focus.

In any given phase of corporate transformation, it is important to limit the number of TIs to three to four. With more than that, there is little likelihood of having enough organizational resources or simplicity to facilitate employee understanding, commitment, and concentration of effort. TIs serve as screening mechanisms for proposed investment in programs and projects to support the transformation. Along the way, TIs, and the programs and projects that are implemented to drive them, are subject to modification and even replacement as their objectives are achieved, as learning from doing disqualifies the continuance of activities, or as new and different challenges.

This means making the tough decisions to net down the focus of the company's execution to a critical few, impactful, high-priority initiatives that everyone will be expected to execute with sustained rigor and courage. These major transformation initiatives are placed in the shaft of the transformation arrow. From direct involvement as principal process architect in dozens of successful CEO-led, enterprise-wide transformations, I have found that transformation initiatives operationalized in a certain manner have the best chance of success.

Here are the bare essentials.

In the shafts of the most successful transformation arrows reside enterprise-wide transformation initiatives, each of which is supported by a limited number of carefully selected areas of focus and outcome metrics, all of which are tied to specific departmental programs of action and individual commitments to action for every soul in every component and at every level in the enterprise. The simple ACT-based framework for operationalizing a transformation initiative is shown in Exhibit 6.9.

Triage to Three to Four Transformation Initiatives

An organization can pursue a maximum of three, possibly four, enterprise-wide transformation initiatives to achieve quantum improvement in a short period of time. Within those top-level initiatives, there needs to be a clear articulation of the areas of intense focus that, when tied to clear outcome metrics, will reveal the distinctive nature of your transformation.

In fact, when it comes to the areas of focus within each initiative, it is strongly recommended that they be strictly limited at the company or departmental level to just three, but not more than four for each initiative. If you start multiplying the number of transformation initiatives times the number of areas of focus, you quickly realize that any more additions will overload

EXHIBIT 6.9   Structure of a Transformation Initiative

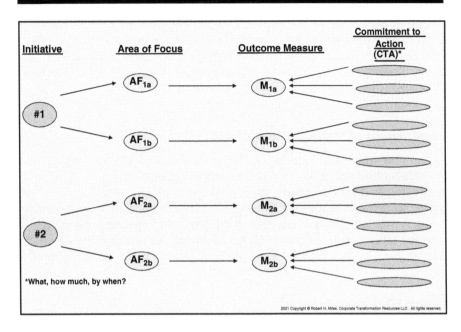

the system. Then the components that you have so carefully crafted to accelerate execution will break down into incremental fragments that will gridlock your people and exhaust your resources.

This is a difficult discipline to follow for transformation leaders and their teams.

Although every enterprise is different, when given the challenge of focusing on three things, most companies typically end up with a similar set of nominal categories for transformation initiatives. One is typically focused on customers and specific customer needs. A second is focused on people and talent management. The third is typically focused on shareholders and financial performance. In some situations, companies have added a fourth transformation initiative that is a critical problem for the business that needs a short-term focus, such as product or service time-to-market, energy efficiency, digitalization, globalization, and so forth. I refer to this as the idiosyncratic initiative that finalizes the tracks on the critical path toward the desired vision state.

Despite the fact that the core three are categorically very similar across successful transforming business organizations, each Transformation Initiative category becomes unique for each company in terms of the two to three Areas of Focus that are selected for each one of them to guide attention and allocate resources to drive them. For example, one company might focus on margins and pricing to drive their financial growth initiative, whereas another might select an acquisition strategy and new product development to achieve its financial growth initiative.

These few, major Transformation Initiatives become the critical link to translate the market- and customer-oriented Strategic Vision into the operations-oriented tactical plans, which every person in the organization will carry as individual commitments. Every employee cannot participate directly in the setting of the Strategic Vision and Success Model. This is the responsibility of senior management. However, it is possible, indeed critical, for every employee to fully engage in how they will personally drive each of the key Transformation Initiatives at their job level and within their sphere of influence.

Transformation Initiative Templates

The set of templates in Exhibit 6.10 illustrate a framework to operationalize the Transformation Initiatives at the enterprise or department level. After this part of the shaft in the Transformation Arrow is clearly articulated, the next step is to achieve alignment among all the subunits; that is, have them complete their versions of the templates and submit them to the Transformation Leader and the SLT for approval. An actual, more detailed TI template for a transforming global "big box" retailer is shown in Exhibit 6.11.

TIs and First Year Results

Exhibit 6.12 below, which summarizes comparisons made in Chapter 3 when the ACT methodology was first introduced, reveals how the Transformation Initiatives line up with first-year results in typical ACT-based transformations. This is what is meant by the definition of Transformation as *"A few well-*

EXHIBIT 6.10   Transformation Initiative Templates

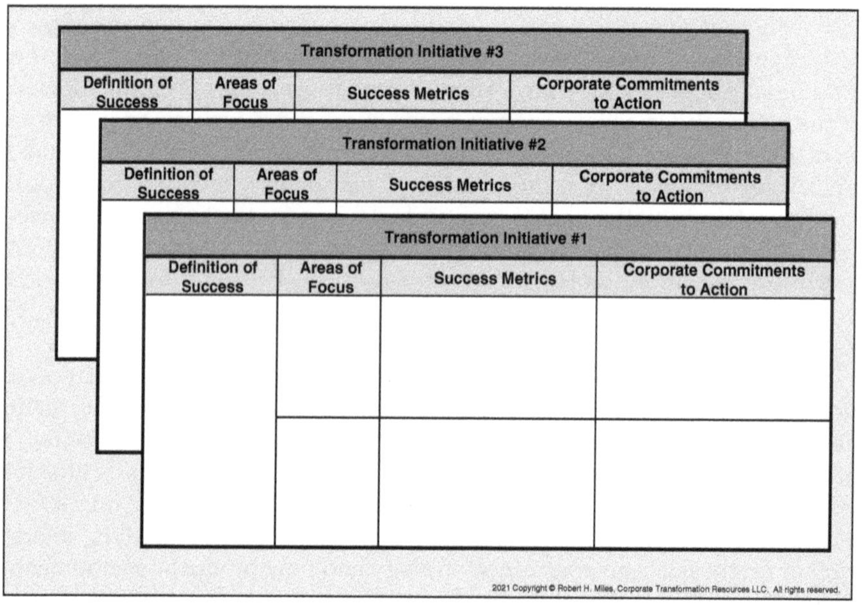

EXHIBIT 6.11   Operationalizing the Initiatives: Retail Example

Customer Focus Initiative

Vision	Areas of Focus	Success Metrics	Commitments to Action
Become the first choice for technology by focusing on the customers' wants and needs	Enhance Price Perception	• Improve "value" perception (from NPD) • Improve "price" perception (from NPD)	1. Implement marketing
	Improve Customer Experience	• Improve Customer rating (from NPD) • Improve "sales and process" 164% to 195	
	Build Brand	• Create Brand and increase rating (from • Improve "Cu Intent" rating NPD)	

Profitable Growth Initiative

Vision	Areas of Focus	Success Metrics	Commitments to Action
Transform the company into a highly profitable, growth company by designing & implementing a long term financial model that aligns with the company strategy.	Drive Margins	Gross Margin = $1.02B (Target: 22.95% @ $4.44B Sales) EBITDA = $131M (Target: 2.96% @ $4.44B Sales)	1. Analysis on product & services net profitability and determine actions to ensure effective mix and assortment 2. Analyze distribution, lifecycle management, replenishment, and returns processes and implement methods to optimize inventory productivity 3. Optimize expense performance
	Drive Growth	Sales Comps = 7.91% Revenue Increase = 11.54%	1. Expand sales to SoHo & Medium Business 2. Optimize store sales conversion through improved close rates and average revenue per transaction 3. Develop real estate plan to include adjustments in current stores, new properties and concepts

EXHIBIT 6.12   Typical First Year Results on Transformation Initiatives

"Big Box" Retailer

Initiatives...
To make Office Depot the most compelling place to....
• INVEST: Shareholder Value Creation
• SHOP: Customer Satisfaction
• INVEST: Retention and Engagement

First Year Results...
• "Worst Ten" to "Number Two" among S&P500 in Shareholder Value Creation
• 50% decrease in Customer Complaints
• 72% increase in Employee Retention

Global Software Company

Initiatives...
To fundamentally reposition this leading high-tech company in an increasingly competitive global software industry.
• Growth
• Retention
• Profitability

First Year Results...
• 24% increase in revenue
• 41% decrease in voluntary employee turnover
• 290% increase in profitability

Large Electric Utility

Initiatives...
To fundamentally reposition in the context of evolving deregulation and competition
• Business Focus
• Adaptive Culture
• Low Cost Producer
• Empowered People

First Year Results...
• $100MM costs reduction in first year ($400MM in three years)
• Union grievances fell 72% in two years
• 38% increase in employee attitude survey
• 30% reduction in reportable accidents

articulated initiatives targeted for breakthrough performance in a short period of time…"

Next, you will need to use the *Rapid, High-engagement, All-employee Cascade*™ process to help managers and employees at all levels develop corresponding individual Commitments to Action. This will be covered in the next chapter, along with how to translate corporate values into to needed behavior changes by managers and employees at all levels.

The result of these final components of the Transformation Arrow is the creation of a clear and compelling line-of-sight accountability from bottom to top in an organization for driving the Transformation Initiatives and living its Values through behavior changes.

TIPS FOR ORCHESTRATING THE FOCUS PHASE: BUSTING THROUGH GRIDLOCK

- The antidote to organization Gridlock is focus. Focus your organization by setting clear direction and priorities starting at the top and through all levels.
- Do more ON less. Focus everyone on just the critical few things that can contribute the most to speeding your journey to first-year breakthrough results.

BUILDING THE TRANSFORMATION ARROW

Establish a *purpose* and *strategic vision* for the organization that

- Specifies how the company is unique
- Signals an aspiration-driven level of achievement
- Clarifies the general playing field
- Focuses on the customer/stakeholders
- Motivates employees; is clear, simple, and memorable

Translate the strategic vision into a *success model* that

- Targets specific customer, market, and product/service areas
- Provides priorities to guide investment and resource allocation decisions
- Conduct a *total-system diagnosis* of the major *gaps* between the current state of the organization and your desired future state
- Conduct due diligence on your own company to quickly

Shoot for three to four *transformation initiatives*, each with no more than three *areas of focus*, and with specific *outcome metrics*.

Notes

1. Portions of this chapter were adapted in part from Robert H. Miles and Michael Kanazawa, *Big Ideas to Big Results: Leading Corporate* *Transformations in a Disruptive World.* Second Edition, Pearson, 2016; and Robert H. Miles, *Leading Corporate Transformation: A Blueprint*

for Business Renewal, Jossey-Bass Publishers, A Division of John Wiley & Sons, 1997.

2. FranklinCovey, xQ Report Based on Harris Interactive Database, December 2003.

3. EY Beacon Institute and Harvard Business Review Analytics, 2015.

4. For more on strategic vision, refer to Robert H. Miles, "The Strategic Visioning Process," *Leading Corporate Transformation*, Jossey-Bass Publishers, Division of John Wiley & Sons, 1997, pp 217–233.

5. Nordstrom, Inc., 2007, Nordstrom website at www.nordstrom.com.

6. Robert X. Cringely, "Getting Real How Microsoft Plans to Dominate Digital TV." I, Cringely Weekly Column, May 7, 1998.

7. Robert H. Miles, *Leading Corporate Transformation: A Blueprint for Business Renewal*, San Francisco: Jossey-Bass Publishers, A Division of John Wily & Sons, 1997, pp. 35–38.

8. The idea that "performance gaps" serve as major catalysts to organizational learning and change has been around for some time. For a summary of several different approaches refer to Robert H. Miles, *Leading Corporate Transformations: A Blueprint for Business Renewal*, Jossey-Bass Publishers, A Division of John Wiley & Sons, 1997, pp. 33–45.

CHAPTER 7

The Align Phase

When transformation initiatives are brought together with aligned organizational values and behaviors the stage is set for rapid achievement of breakthrough results in terms of both business outcomes and culture change.

As your transformation launch shifts to the Align Phase, you will need to continue the intensive work with your executive team to complete the remaining components of the transformation arrow and ensure that the top three levels of leaders, counting yourself, are fully aligned before asking them to cascade the commitment-setting process rapidly and consistently to all their employees.[1]

Left on your to-do list is the refinement and alignment to the enterprise-wide transformation initiatives of each *area of focus* and *success metric* by division or department. Afterwards, all members of the leadership team need to set their own *commitments to action* to support each of the three to four transformation initiatives. In addition, the transformation game plan is not complete until you identify the few important values that support the transformation initiatives and to which *behavior change commitments* must be made, starting with you and your leadership team.

Finally, once all members of your team have developed their aligned performance and behavioral change commitments, there is a need to pause for a serious *Stop Doing* exercise, as well as for your personal assessment of the earnestness of your team members before cascading the transformation to all managers and employees.

Let's take these critical elements of the Align Phase one at a time.

ABSOLUTE ALIGNMENT

As we have discussed, fragmented, under-resourced lists of ideas overlaid on an already overtaxed system are persistent nemeses along the path to transformation. This is what happens when you don't stick to a limited set of primary initiatives with full alignment at the top.

As the senior vice president of IT in one of our large retail company transformations has pointed out, "If you're not uncomfortable with how tight

DOI: 10.4324/9781003272724-7

the initiatives are, they're not tight enough. The tighter the initiatives, the bigger impact they can have because people and resources will be leveraged to their best."

INDIVIDUAL COMMITMENTS TO ACTION

The transition from transformation planning to doing involves setting individual *Commitments to Action (CTAs)*. The entire organization needs to engage in the process of developing and committing to act on a limited set of individual commitments that are in alignment with the transformation initiatives relevant to each employee's job scope.

The end goal of engaging the full organization in the process is to generate a situation in which all people are able to set specific commitments to action that are aligned to drive the overall results. These commitments need to be relevant for their level of contribution, aligned to support the top objectives, and things they were able to help design. The commitments need to be "their" promises to support the transformation.

This step is often nonexistent in strategy communications sessions, which typically take place as big kickoff events with lots of fanfare and little engagement or follow-through for results. In contrast, the odds of a person following through with excellence on commitments that they helped develop are much higher than just completing tasks assigned by others.

In performance management and goal-setting processes at many companies, the goals are set only between an employee and his or her direct manager, usually with no specific understanding about the company strategy and without any dialogue with the rest of the peer team on what is needed from that individual. The only documents discussed at an individual goal-setting session might be a copy of last year's performance review and a draft of the next year's performance review document for the individual. Such sessions usually devolve into a perfunctory administrative task of filling in blanks rather than having a real dialogue about priorities, personal commitments, and job design for the coming year.

In the work on a transformation project at a global technology company, senior executives thought they had this aced. They believed that each employee at the company routinely set his or her individual business commitments at the beginning of each calendar year, to be reviewed semi-annually as part of the performance management process. But when we examined the company's actual process in action, most individuals didn't get around to setting their commitments until June, just in the nick of time of their semiannual performance appraisal!

The fix that was introduced with their transformation launch was to simultaneously hook the commitment setting and performance appraisal setting across the entire organization during the transformation cascade rollout. Using the ACT-based *Rapid, All-employee, High-engagement Cascade*™ (discussed in detail in the next chapter), they were able to get individual commitments drafted, peer-reviewed, and approved in *one* high-engagement setting at each level in the businesses and functions. This enabled them to quickly achieve alignment from top to bottom in the organization and immediately ramp the cycle of transformation execution and learning for the full performance year.

Many executives don't appreciate the need to do this – or are simply unaware that it is possible to do this – until they've missed their first-year transformation initiative targets by wide margins.[2]

Alignment of Commitments Across "Silos"

Once the leadership team has worked through the steps to effectively confront reality, set the direction, and create transformation initiatives, many managers feel like the commitment to action part of the process is a break from the teamwork and a chance to take the team's plan and run to daylight with just their piece of the transformation. To some extent, they are correct. Personal commitments to action must be set in every subunit and by every person in the organization. However, even with all the senior leaders having been intensively involved together in developing the transformation game plan, it is very easy for their commitments to get out of alignment across the business and functional groups.

With a simple exercise of writing each senior executive's commitments and those of their subunits on index cards and posting them on a wall, they all can see how their collective commitments mesh. So, it is critical before rollout to vet the transformation game plan with the next level of leadership, which ACT refers to as the Extended Leadership Team (ELT), whose members make up the leadership teams of each of the company's business units and functional departments.

But more than that, members of the Senior Leadership Team (SLT) should go through a quick round of exchanges with their peers of the commitments they have worked out with their own teams. Even though most of their perspectives will have been aired in earlier transformation dialogues with their peers, some interdependencies inevitably get overlooked, and gaps in coverage can surprise well into the transformation planning process. For this reason, a final planning meeting of the SLT that is dedicated to resolving dependencies and closing gaps is always a good idea. This brief pause doesn't have to be elaborate because the senior team has worked closely on all the earlier launch steps.

This simple exercise at the end of the transformation planning process invariably surfaces misalignments and unrecognized interdependencies, which can quickly be addressed. Often there are gaps in coverage that if not filled before rollout will retard performance during the Execute Phase.

To drive home the importance of alignment from top to bottom in an organization, consider the reflections of a CEO who was attempting to transform a perfectly good basic materials company into a great one. Looking back over the first year of his successful corporate transformation, he concluded that,

> *I think the business challenge that the ACT process handles beautifully is the congealing of the top leadership team on what you want done and then cascading it down so it is communicated to every employee.*

His CFO, who had partnered with us on arranging the process architecture to launch the transformation during that "good to great" challenge, chimed in similarly:

A by-product of this process is that when you require a business leader -- whether at the Senior Leadership Team or quarry manager level -- to make presentations to their own people about their goals and commitments, they are really publicly stating what "we are going to accomplish." It makes those people realize they have to act as mentors or leaders. It's not just a selfish game anymore. These people to whom they've made the speeches are now watching to see if they are going to walk the talk.

Where Should Lightning Strike?

Another pitfall to avoid in setting commitments to action (CTAs) at the top is the tendency to assign sole functional responsibility for each transformation initiative. This traditional approach to goal setting may sometimes be sufficient during steady-state conditions. But when your organization has to rise to a transformation challenge, all hands, meaning all organizational components, are needed behind all of the few, major transformation initiatives.

In contrast, leadership teams often mistakenly identify the "people" initiative as one that the human resources (HR) department should own and execute. However, if the VPs of all staff departments and business units do not sign up for individual commitments to improve the quality of people on their team, the people initiative targeted for quantum improvements in a short period of time will be doomed to disappoint.

Successful people strategies cannot be owned only by HR; they need to have full commitment and active involvement from the Senior Leadership Team, which represents all components of the organization. Every leader on that team should have a reasonable set of personal commitments to action to support that type of initiative. A general manager can make a commitment to deliver the key programs HR will develop, such as 360 reviews, improved recruiting and interviewing processes, or succession planning. This way, when a manager's team is asked to get involved in the initiatives, it is to support their boss and their team's goals, not just to respond to being asked to do something by another department. This holds true for all other types of initiatives. Responsibility for growth, quality, or product development, as further examples, must be squarely borne by all members of the leadership team and the parts of the organization for which they are responsible, not just by the department that specializes in a particular initiative.

As a general rule, then, *all* members of the Senior Leadership Team should be responsible, albeit with varying weights, for *all* the transformation initiatives. Each leader should be able to get behind at least some of each initiative's areas of focus and action programs. All the levels and components of the organization can have an impact on the growth and people initiatives, as examples; not just the sales and HR departments, respectively. Indeed, even the lowest-level job holder in an enterprise can find legitimate and useful ways to formulate personal commitments to drive these and other transformation initiatives. So, make sure members of the leadership team don't fall into the "this is my turf" trap. When corporate transformation is the challenge, each member of the Senior Leadership Team will need all the help they can get from their peers in charge of other parts of the enterprise.

Working on the alignment of the transformation initiatives up front and across the organization will ensure that team members in different work groups will all be working under priorities and tactics that are mutually reinforcing. Silo conflicts are reduced, and greater execution results.

ALIGNMENT OF VALUES

Another indispensable element in generating and sustaining alignment is the living of *shared Company Values*. Every day, people in the organization will be faced with making decisions that will either move the organization forward or not. Living by a core set of values allows individuals to make decisions on situations that haven't been addressed before and to stay in alignment with the transformation as they make those decisions, when you and others aren't around to help them think through things. Values should be tied to specific, desired behavior changes as part of the transformation.

Bedrock values – the ones you might find in the "scout codes" – begin to be developed in employees, not when they arrive in an organization, but when they start out their lives. They are the result of the confluence of parental supervision, role modeling by respected peers and adults, and trial and effort in the real world. These are the kinds of things that definitely ought to be screened for when people are selected for employment in a company. Without such traits, which are part and parcel of being a good person and a good citizen, no organization can sustain itself, much less flourish.

However, an additional values dimension is needed in organizations attempting a transformation. In this dimension are the enterprise-specific values selected by the leadership team, which are aligned with and that uniquely support their transformation initiatives. Such values are needed to guide the behavior changes required at all levels to ensure transformation success. The best results on this dimension are achieved when the chosen company values are tied directly to the three to four transformation initiatives.

To illustrate, let's take the example discussed earlier in the book. During the turnaround of the global "big box" retailer following a disallowed merger with a rival, the new CEO and executive team eventually selected three primary initiatives to launch the revitalization of their company. They said to all constituencies that they wanted the company to become the "most compelling place in the industry to invest, shop, and work." Underlying these catchy categories, they developed a limited set of areas of focus and metrics to focus and drive their turnaround:

Invest – Shareholder value creation

Shop – Customer satisfaction

Work – Employee retention and reengagement

When they turned to select the values that made the most sense to emphasize during the transformation effort, they had a long list that had been posted in all the conference rooms by the previous regime. After some structured dialogue, the team relatively quickly decided that an emphasis on three values made the most sense and could probably make the greatest contribution during the first year, given the selected initiatives. The values they singled out for special attention were

1. *Respect for the Individual* - The company's employee base was quite diverse, so this value was believed to be a critical factor in achieving the "best place to work" initiative.
2. *Fanatical Customer Service* – During the long wait for approval of its acquisition by a rival retailer, which was ultimately denied by the Department of Justice, the company had lost its focus on the customer. Driving value in customer service was viewed as critical to creating the best place to shop.
3. *Excellence in Execution* – During all the turmoil, the company and its employees had also lost their focus on execution. This value was designed to help encourage the restoration of excellence in execution, which, in turn, would contribute to their becoming the best place to invest in their industry category.

Exhibit 7.1 shows how the transformation initiatives, outcome metrics, and values were clearly aligned, making the business drivers and values mutually reinforcing. This alignment greatly simplifies and focuses both operational and personnel or cultural efforts on the same initiatives. It is easier for people at all levels to understand, remember, and execute.

By the end of the first year of execution, the retailer achieved the following breakthrough results on its transformation initiatives:

EXHIBIT 7.1   The Values-Performance Nexus

Values	Respect for the Individual	Fanatical Customer Service	Excellence in Execution
	↕	↕	↕
	The Most Compelling Place to…		
Transformation Initiatives	Work	Shop	Invest
Area of Focus	Employee Retention and Engagement	Customer Satisfaction	Shareholder Value Creation
First-Year Outcomes	72% Improvement in Employee Retention	50% Reduction in Customer Complaints	From "Worst 10" to "#2" among S&P 500 on Shareholder Value Creation

The CEO later reflected that it was, "a proven methodology that says if you apply these tools, you can accelerate the engagement of the whole entire organization. I just became single-mindedly focused on it.[3]

The Values-Performance Nexus

After the core values are identified, they need to be anchored in individual commitments to behavior changes, initially at the top, starting with the CEO and his or her direct reports (SLTs), their direct reports (ELTs) and then throughout the entire enterprise.

When transformation initiatives are brought together with aligned organizational values in the performance management system of a transforming enterprise, the stage is set (as shown in Exhibit 7.2) for rapid achievement of breakthrough results in terms of both business outcomes and culture change.[4]

STRUCTURING WIDESPREAD COMMITMENT

To support an accelerated corporate transformation, individual CTAs must be made by everyone in the organization – yes, everyone from the Transformation Leader to the last person in the door. And this must be accomplished simply, smoothly, and rapidly once the leadership team has completed the transformation arrow. How to accomplish this rapidly – actually *in a single team sitting* at each organizational level – will be described in detail in the next chapter. Here it is important to demystify the apparatus that ACT has successfully deployed over and over to structure everyone's CTAs.

EXHIBIT 7.2   Corporate Transformation Success: A Balancing Act

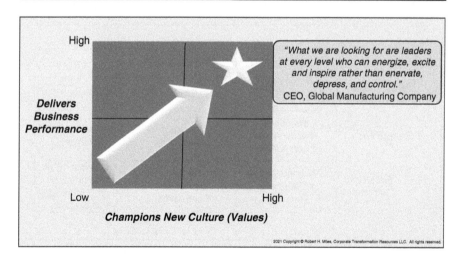

"What we are looking for are leaders at every level who can energize, excite and inspire rather than enervate, depress, and control."
CEO, Global Manufacturing Company

High

Low

High

Delivers Business Performance

Champions New Culture (Values)

EXHIBIT 7.3   Individual Commitments to Action and Behavioral Change

Performance Commitments to Action
Performance Appraisal - Example

Team Member Performance Appraisal

Name:	Division:
Title:	Location:
Supervisor:	Title:

Assessment: Year ___   Q1 ☐   Q2 ☐   Q3 ☐   Annual ☐

Corporate Initiative	Title:	Areas of Focus
Profitable Growth	1	Drive Margin
	2	Drive Growth

Area of Focus	Commitments to Action	Metrics	Time Frame	Comments	Rating*

· S=Superior, ER=Exceeded Requirements, MR=Meets Requirements, NI=Needs Improvement, U=Unsatisfactory

Behavioral Change Commitments

Team Member Performance Appraisal

Value	Behavioral Change Commitment	Comments	Rating*
Respect			
Play to Win			
Customer First			

Supervisor's Comments:

Supervisor's Rating [   ]

Reviewed with Team Member

| Team Member: | Date: |
| Supervisor: | Date: |

Team Member Comments:

Believe it or not, you need to use the same structured format to capture and record the CEO's commitments as we deploy to first-line employees. It couldn't be simpler.

Recall that you not only want to set performance commitments to drive the transformation initiatives, but also *Behavioral Change Commitments* to live the values that support the Purpose and Strategic Vision. To capture the CTAs of every person in the enterprise, use the templates shown in Exhibit 7.3. Start by completing the CEO's or Transformation Leader's CTAs and then systematically but quickly work all the way down through the organization. Each individual first completes one version of the top form for each transformation initiative before completing the form at the bottom for his or her Behavior Change Commitments. The conveyer for this is the *Rapid, High-engagement, All-Employee Cascade*™ (to be discussed in detail in the next chapter).

When filling out the CTA forms, it is useful to offer a simple set of guidelines – an old but always reliable checklist. Ask everyone to make their commitments S-M-A-R-T.

S: SPECIFIC

Is the CTA clear, understandable, and well defined?

M: MEASURABLE

Can the results of the CTA be quantified?

A: ALIGNED

Does the CTA fit with higher-level and adjacent CTAs?

R: RELEVANT

Is the CTA the best way that I can contribute to the achievement of higher-level CTAs, and do I have the authority, knowledge, and skill to fulfill the CTA?

T: TIME-BASED

Have I given the CTA a completion date?

The First "Stop Doing" Pause

So far, you've used structured dialogue in a compressed format in Launch Phase meetings to confront reality and to develop Purpose, Strategic Vision, and Success Model components of the Transformation Arrow that are motivating, focusing, and challenging. You've worked closely with your team to articulate only a few major Transformation Initiatives, each with a limited set of Areas of Focus to drive attention, resource allocation, and execution. You've also feathered in agreement on a few enterprise-wide Values and used them to obtain behavior change, in addition to performance commitments from your leaders.

The last step before aligning your organization with a major transformation launch or strategy execution effort involves deciding what *not* to do. This is the step many Transformation Leaders skip only to pay for dearly later in the Execute Phase. Making the tough trade-offs about what to stop so that resources can be allocated to the most important initiatives is not easy. But it is essential to moving the organization into a doing-more-ON-less mode for transformation success.

Think of your first "stop doing" exercise with your leadership team as an essential, last whistle stop on the tracks leading to full cascade and full execution. It is a major transformation step, but it can be so simple. Just assemble your leadership team. Give them advance notice that unless this step is successful, they'll end up having to do more *with* less in leading their parts of the corporate transformation. In addition, ask them to prepare by working with their department team on identifying and prioritizing any of their activities that do not lie on the critical path of the transformation game plan.

Instruct them that anything is fair game but that most progress in their triage effort will come from focusing on projects and programs in their own subunits over which they have direct control. Tell them not to forget standing committees and meetings, procedures and approvals, and reports.

Make sure when you convene the SLT, whose members presumably have run all of this for full discussion with their own leadership team, you properly set up the Stop Doing meeting by reminding everyone about the *safe passage* rules, the *structured dialogue* guidelines, and the *tablework* procedures. That will help you keep emotions in check as your executives struggle with identifying give-ups that they otherwise might prefer to protect. (The Focus and Align Phases were adapted from GE's famous WorkOut! Program in which I participated as a senior consultant.)

From the tablework with your SLT, capture all the nominated candidates and then distill the candidates for elimination into the following categories: meetings, reports, processes/approvals, and projects. Write each candidate for elimination on a Post-It.

Then, within each category, rate each candidate for elimination on two criteria:

1. Control:

   1. The idea is within my own personal control to stop doing;
   2. The idea requires my own group or department to stop doing; or
   3. The idea requires people, groups, or departments outside my own area to stop doing.

2. Importance:

   1. Small effect on efficiency/performance
   2. Moderate effect on efficiency/performance
   3. Substantial effect on efficiency/performance

Make the ratings transparent by posting them for all to see. It should be easy to agree on which are the most critical tasks to stop doing. Without some kind of structure and process, getting the key leaders of your transformation to put their pet projects and sacred cows on the chopping block would be quite challenging.

And be forewarned: Essential as it is to have a rigorous "Stop Doing" exercise before shifting into the Cascade and Execute Phases, it will not be the only time you will need to do this exercise. People are timid at first to give up things to which they are personally committed and for which they have been rewarded. Early in a transformation process, many are not convinced that the leader will stay the course. So, you may have to conduct repeats during the first year of the Execute Phase and certainly one before you re-plan and re-launch your second year of transformation. In general, the more you hold people accountable for results on the key transformation initiatives, the more interested everyone will become and the more aggressive they will be in removing low-impact projects from their agendas that don't fall on the transformation critical path.

Put Your Money Where Your Game Plan Is

This book began with a definition of transformation as "A few well-articulated initiatives targeted for breakthrough performance in a short period of time – in a sea of necessary incremental improvements."

After the three to four transformation initiatives have been agreed upon and the Stop Doing exercise has been harvested, but well before the initiation of the Execute Phase, there must be a fundamental realignment of the budget and reallocation of resources that reflects their importance in the scheme of the transformation challenge. To become treated as being real, the new transformation initiatives must impact the way investment decisions are made to reflect the new priorities they represent.

Too often, the transformation game plan and new strategy and success model are not aligned with operating budgets. In some companies, the strategic planning process is done by the CEO and the Senior Leadership Team, budgeting is run separately by finance, and performance goals and management are programs administered by human resources. In addition, it is insufficient to create an "incremental" budget for the corporate transformation initiatives, in which only a small percentage of the total operating budget is set aside to fund these key initiatives. Such underfunding will surely result in an increased overlay of initiatives that add to gridlock and fail to properly incentivize alignment and commitment to the new transformation initiatives. Nothing less than a full alignment of the purpose, strategic vision, success model, values, budgets, transformation initiatives, and individual commitments to action will provide the organization-wide focus and sustained energy to break the pattern of continuing to add to task overload and organizational gridlock.

The Bottom Line on Alignment

If your objective is to generate strategic alignment quickly, which is what is required to transform a company or a major component of it, you need absolute alignment starting at the top. The issue posed by just a few recalcitrant executives has been identified as one of the major inhibitors to successful transformation. If you have any misalignment at the top, it will only become magnified as it goes down through the organization. Again, big leaders cast large shadows! And if you encourage one department to try to "change the world" while permitting another to focus on the "same old, same old," you will be setting up both departments – as well as the transformation you hope to achieve – for failure. So be careful about considering plans that get parts of the organization out of sync or even working at odds with each other.

By the time your transformation process reaches the end of the Align Phase, you should be aware of a few potentially derailing behaviors of still uncommitted senior executives. Skeptical team members might have been willing to participate in the early launch activities involving the development of a new purpose, strategic vision, and success model. Given a strong commitment by the Transformation Leader, savvy managers will understand that they cannot avoid participating in the development of the new direction. And participation does afford them the opportunity to influence the transformation game plan. But, although they may play well on the front end of this creative process, they often avoid putting all their cards on the table. Instead, they play a game of poker – watching others turn over their cards first so that they can strengthen their hand before the time comes when major resource allocation decisions and commitments to organization changes are made.

Another behavior pattern to avoid full commitment to the transformation game plan is to argue for a continuation of "baseline funding" while making only incremental investments on the Transformation Initiatives. Incrementalists often argue that because most of the revenue or profits are derived from the current business, disruption needs to be minimized. Unfortunately, the perpetuation of these tactics in the face of major transformational challenges ensures the continued pursuit of the status quo. The critical few transformation initiatives, by contrast, are targeted for quantum improvements in a relatively short period of time. These initiatives are not intended to be new incremental projects.

Finally, as you wind down your Align Phase watch out for their suggestion that you conduct a pilot test first! Granted, there are many situations in which it makes sense to hold the main body of an improvement effort in abeyance, often involving a beta sight and an extended delay for a year or even more. *But when faced with an existential transformation challenge involving a clear and imminent opportunity or danger to the enterprise, the solution is more one of speed to execution coupled with intensive learning-from-doing.* This action learning from execution mode makes it possible to quickly award early wins and equally quickly terminate early failures to redirect resources to major initiatives on the critical path of the transformation game plan. That is what an ACT-based transformation was uniquely designed to do. More about how in the chapter on the Execute Phase.

Gut Check on Commitment

As the Transformation Leader, you must challenge the full organization to align with the major strategic shifts that the team has committed to achieve. This starts at the very top. Active resisters from the onset of transformation planning must eventually be confronted before the shift into the Engage and Execute Phases, and, if necessary, removed from their posts. For executive leaders on your team perched on the fence – somewhere between tentatively withholding support from or passively championing the new agenda – give them an opportunity to participate in designing the transformation game plan, working within the proven process architecture that we have been discussing. Allow them to provide input, share their ideas, shape the initiatives, and plan the rollout. But before moving into the employee Engage Phase, circle back with each one of them to determine if they are solidly on board. This step is critical to be able to roll out the leader-led part of your transformation.

At this stage in your ACT-based transformation, the Launch Phase is complete and you are entering into what most executives, managers, supervisors, and employees regard as by far the most exciting part of your transformation: the *Rapid, High-Engagement, All-Employee Cascade*™. When most Transformation Leaders look in the rear view mirror, they see a completed Launch Phase roadmap that looks very similar to the one shown in Exhibit 7.4.

TIPS FOR THE ALIGN PHASE

Achieve *absolute alignment* from top to bottom:

- Quickly address even small deviations from the focus at the top as these get magnified going down – senior executives cast big shadows over the division below them.
- Drive accountability throughout the entire organization through setting individual commitments to action at all levels.
- Restack all priorities top to bottom to ensure your transformation initiatives get the "unfair" amount of attention and focus they require for success.

EXHIBIT 7.4 Typical ACT Launch Roadmap

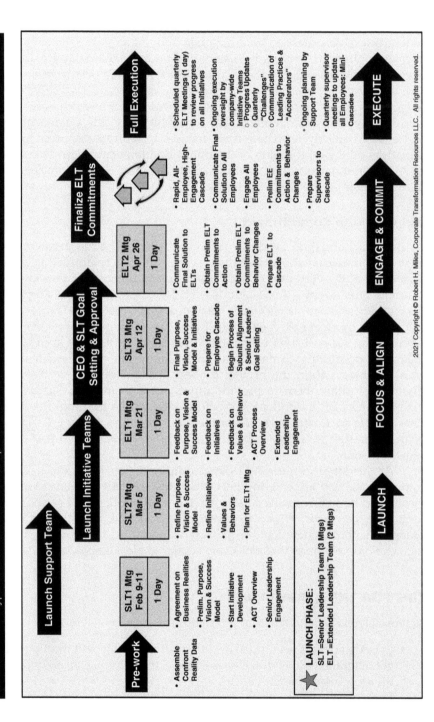

- Reset investment and operating budget levels to align with the transformation initiative priorities.
- Establish clear guidelines for resource allocation that will enable you to quickly identify through action learning and eliminate projects that are not on the transformation critical path.

Align values and behaviors:

- Select a few values that strategically align with the transformation initiatives.
- Anchor the values in individuals' behavior change commitments at all levels in the organization.
- Pause for a "Stop Doing" exercise to align priorities and resource allocation. More than one if necessary.
- Quickly address and handle any situations in which leaders will not align fully. They won't be up to the task of cascading the transformation in a clear, aligned, and engaging manner.

Notes

1. Portions of this chapter were adapted in part from Robert H. Miles and Michael Kanazawa, *Big Ideas to Big Results: Leading Corporate Transformations in a Disruptive World*. Second Edition, Pearson, 2016; and Robert H. Miles, *Leading Corporate Transformation: A Blueprint for Business Renewal*, Jossey-Bass Publishers, A Division of John Wiley & Sons, 1997.

2. For a more complete treatment of the ACT-based Rapid, High-engagement, All-employee Cascade, refer to Robert H. Miles, "Beyond the Age of Dilbert: Accelerating Corporate Transformations by Rapidly Engaging All Employees," Organization Dynamics, Special Edition, Summer 2001.

3. For a more complete treatment of Values, refer to an earlier work of Robert H. Miles, *Leading Corporate Transformation: Blueprint for Business Renewal*, San Francisco, Jossey-Bass Publishers, a Division of John Wiley & Sons, 1997, pp. 51–53.

4. Brian O'Connor, "Anatomy of a Turnaround: How Bruce Nelson Revived Office Depot," Fasttrack Magazine, Summer 2002, pp. 42–47.

CHAPTER 8

The Engage Phase

"How can you engage and energize thousands of employees within a matter of weeks?"

RAPIDLY ENGAGING THE FULL ORGANIZATION

Leaders don't generally raise that question because they are not aware that such a feat can be accomplished in a rapid, reliable manner. But it's one of the major questions they should be asking when challenged with taking charge and launching the next major phase in an organization. Instead, many transformations stall at this point in the roadmap because the great ideas and strategies constructed at the top never make it far enough down in the company to have a palpable impact on employees and customers, which is where it matters most.[1]

Past efforts, they recall, have taken months, if not years to roll out from top to bottom. Many of such failed attempts to engage employees in a rapid, organization-wide manner are implemented as one-off programs sponsored by staff departments, not integrated into normal business operations or transformation game plan. No wonder a recent study of American workers revealed that only one in ten employees has a clear line of sight between their job tasks and their company's goals. Moreover, only half of the surveyed employees felt that there was any follow-through with discipline from above on key priorities.[2]

Too quick to delegate, many executives simply watch the Execute Phase wither after the pass off to consultants or staff specialists.

The problem with these plodding approaches is that by the time the message reaches the full organization, the top has already moved to new challenges and launched new strategies, putting the system out of alignment. And as you'll see, a message delivered by anyone other than the direct manager will not drive execution down to the next level.

The key to enabling employee engagement and performance success is that such efforts must be encompassed within the context of an overall transformation game plan; one that is leader-led.

Leader-led Employee Engagement

The largest immediate boost in performance that companies get following an ACT-based transformation process is a dramatic increase in employee

DOI: 10.4324/9781003272724-8

engagement. Does that surprise you? It's surprising to many leaders. Creating a fully engaged workforce, one where individuals bring their best every day is a necessary element to generating great results. An engaged workforce is one in which people have passion for their roles and continually look for ways to contribute to their organization's performance.

Every leader hopes to attract self-starting people who are aligned and engaged with the organization's purpose, strategic vision, key initiatives, and culture. Indeed, if we do only a halfway decent job of hiring, our organizations should be filled with high-energy, creative-thinking people, who make up high-performance teams that are driving big results. But many of those bright eyes soon turn dim with experience in a given organization. Many of the great employees we hire soon begin to feel underutilized, marginalized, and disengaged all too soon. Indeed, a study of 840,000 employees of multinational companies revealed that employee satisfaction begins dropping at six months, and then it bottoms out at about three to five years.[3] Those in leadership positions are clearly not engaging their teams effectively. Moreover, even the best of employees can get left behind if they are not actively engaged by their leaders when the organization needs to make transformational shift.

QUANTUM LEAPS IN ENGAGEMENT

For several years, a large, public utility company facing impending deregulation struggled to generate a more competitive and high-performing workforce. The chart in Exhibit 8.1 clearly shows that during the three years prior to the ACT-based intervention, very little overall movement occurred on various dimensions of employee satisfaction and engagement. The year immediately following the launch of a high-engagement, ACT-based transformation, quantum improvements were achieved across all dimensions of measured employee satisfaction and engagement throughout the 92 unionized plants in the company's portfolio.[4]

Union officials and front-line employees had become fully engaged as part of the ACT-based *Rapid, High-engagement, All-employee Cascade*™ in thinking through how to operate their local area of responsibility differently under the company's new transformation initiative guidelines, rather than simply being told as usual what to do and how to do it.

"Back in Black" Friday

What does a quantum leap in employee engagement look like, and what does it do for you in leading a transformation effort? At a national retail company, sales had been on a constant downward slide for five years. In fact, the company believed that its brand had been forgotten and it might need to change its name. There were also big challenges coming from new competitors and business model shifts. It was about halfway through the performance year when the new CEO and COO decided to apply the ACT process to accelerate a transformation. (It is noteworthy that while many Transformation Leaders tend to prefer to launch at the beginning of a whole performance year, this new

EXHIBIT 8.1   ACT-based Employment Engagement Leap

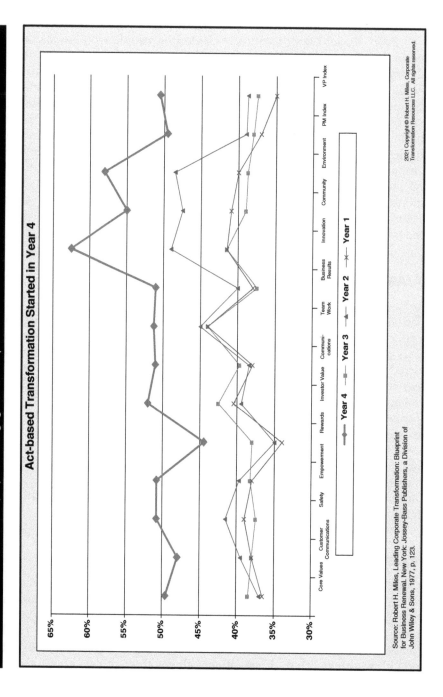

Act-based Transformation Started in Year 4

Source: Robert H. Miles, Leading Corporate Transformation: Blueprint for Business Renewal. New York: Jossey-Bass Publishers, a Division of John Wiley & Sons, 1977, p. 123.

CEO-COO team decided that their situation was so urgent when they took over that they decided to lift the tent pegs at mid-year by launching their ACT-based "taking charge" transformation.)

For retailers, Black Friday refers to the Friday after Thanksgiving, the day that many retailers finally go beyond break-even profitability – from being in the "red" (losing money) to being in the "black" (making money). It is typically the single day of the year that has the highest sales. It is a huge indicator for retailers each year on how they are performing overall. After engaging the full organization from the top executives down through the cashiers and warehouse staff in early August, the company experienced a large jump in employee engagement, taking them from the competitive bottom quartile to the top half compared to similar companies.

That leap in engagement felt good to the executives, but would it translate into results? By the time Black Friday results were being tallied, they knew the answer was yes. With no major increase in mass advertising spending, the company had generated the largest sales day in its history (including the heydays that had long since passed). It put them on track to have the first profitable full year and full year of positive year-over-year growth in same-store sales in the recent past. What had changed? The marketing and merchandising teams had been engaged by the new executives for weekly creative thinking sessions, store employees were allowed to prioritize serving customers over taking inventory, and everyone felt as though they had some say in how to do their jobs better every day. At that point, there had been no rebranding and no massive ad spending to bring customers back – there had just been a simple re-engagement and re-focusing of the entire team.

Following the close of the year, members of the management team were gathered to discuss the great results, when one executive asked what the team thought was the key: one of the operations staff managers put it best this way, "Maybe that's what happens when you get 14,000 people engaged and excited again."

Employee Engagement Is not Barbeque

But not all engagement attempts bear such bountiful fruit. One ill-fated attempt to restore rank-and-file employee engagement involved a planned "evangelical" event. It was conducted by an iconic high-tech company in Silicon Valley during the height of the 1990s boom. The company had well-branded products, but more standard alternatives had virtually devoured its business. Barely clinging to a 3% domestic market share, executives were in a panic. They were hoping that one major attention-gathering event shared by all headquarters employees would be sufficient to re-focus and re-energize their dis-engaged workforce.

Plans were carefully laid to transport all employees to a local fairground. The leaders rented the fleets of yellow school buses from several nearby schools to transport employees to and from the event. When the buses had delivered students to school in the morning, and when they had to pick them up when classes ended, set the start and stop limits for the company's planned event.

The Cascade venue was organized around a big-screen, multimedia appeal to all hands, which outlined the new vision for the company, sketched the broad outlines of some new initiatives, and called for a return to the values and behaviors that had once made the company great. Ranging somewhere between a religious tent revival and a Big Ten pep rally, the event amounted to a great exhortation by executive leaders for all employees to perform differently and better on the job, all reinforced by lots of pyrotechnics and applause. Employees were treated with lunch before boarding buses to return to the headquarters.

A week later, I happened to catch one of the company's VPs coming out of a store in downtown Palo Alto where I got to ask him what he thought of his company's Cascade kickoff event. He paused, smiled, and with a twinkle in his eyes he replied, "All I can recall with clarity is the quality of the barbecue!" During the next few months, the company's transformation began to take the shape of the failed transformation in the Exhibit in the Preface. Lots of excitement upfront, but little follow-through. Shortly thereafter, the CEO, the second in close progression, was replaced by the Board.

Observing failed attempts like this one led to the design of a comprehensive but streamlined vehicle for rapidly creating "leaders at all levels" in a transforming enterprise. The ACT approach to employee rollout of a transformation game plan is simple, streamlined, and fast; an intervention that combines the benefits of employee training and communication with engagement, alignment, and performance management *in one sitting*.

The following section highlights some general design elements of this proven Cascade architecture that enables leaders to create rapid and effective engagement, which then leads directly to formal commitment and accountability. Some of the elements we explore with you may sound trivial. But success with employee engagement comes from the cumulative impact of a few very monumentally magnificent trivial choices.[5]

CASCADING HIGH ENGAGEMENT

Imagine that an executive team has been working collaboratively through the ACT steps to confront reality, create a strategy, and determine the focus for the organization. How do you get the rest of the organization engaged? Surprisingly, it is the same method for how the top team became engaged. Supervisors with their employees experienced firsthand and made sense of the transformation game plan during their Cascade meetings in which was embedded a similar round of tablework modules, all based on the same principles of "safe passage" and "structured dialogue," much the same as the senior leadership team had used to create the transformation game plan. Only more streamlined. It's this simple:

- Structure the Cascade encounter around the elements in the Transformation Arrow. Devote a module to each element in the Arrow.
- Pause after the opening presentation in each module for the immediate supervisor to explain its relevance to their team before sharing the Commitments to Action (CTAs) they had made to their manager in the previous Cascade session one level above.
- Allow a few precious moments for personal reflection. (What does this transformation initiative, for example, mean for me? For us? How can we support our supervisor's commitments?)

- Open the session for structured dialogue and feedback.
- Challenge and expect individuals to translate the plans into personal CTAs. ("What does it mean for me?")
- Instruct each team member to record his or her preliminary personal CTAs before sharing them with his or her supervisor and team members.
- Finalize these CTAs between the supervisor and each team member within five days so that the member can swiftly set the next level Cascade session in which the process is repeated with his or her direct reports down through the bottom organizational level.

This sequence of steps may be performed in the local setting, or dozens of supervisor-employee teams can be sitting in a large hotel banquet room setting, each at their own team's table. The latter option affords the opportunity for teams to be sampled in the larger forum to share how they planned to align with the new transformation initiatives and behavior change commitments. In the larger forum, there is a certain element of theater that reinforces employee engagement and commitment, which is lost if the first Cascade event for an individual is given away to a long-distance social media activity.

Specific illustrations of these modules will be provided later in the chapter.

Critical Importance of Dialogue

As we discussed before, dialogue is a critical element of successful engagement and commitment. Yet there is a natural tendency among executives and staffers when pressed for time to cut dialogue out of important meetings and other forums. As I've said, ACT uses the same form of structured dialogue to bring employees aboard during well-defined Cascade meetings as I described earlier with the work of the Senior Leadership Team and Extended Leadership Team during the Launch Phase to craft and refine the corporate transformation game plan and to bring their subunit leadership teams aboard. Even the senior-most executives don't get it until they become engaged in the ACT-based manner.

Leading the Cascade

In the *Rapid, High-engagement, All-employee Cascade*™ process, these same managers are called into action to actively lead execution of the transformation initiatives in their part of the organization, no matter what level or standing they have. And to do this right, each person in a leadership position needs to be willing to create a setting in which even the lowest-ranking or most recently arrived employee can have a big impact. Such leaders need to do this by first stepping up and out onto the limb to set bold commitments to support the major transformation initiatives, as well as commitments to visible behavior changes to live the values.

Then they need to set up their own rapid, high-engagement Cascade event using the principles we have been discussing to make it safe for their direct reports to take risks to change the status quo and set new and different commitments to drive the transformation game in their level and sphere of influence. This is a tall order, so you have to get the Engage Phase right. That's how you'll achieve quantum improvements across the enterprise in a short period of time.

Enough about broad Cascade concepts to drive your transformation game plan. Let's now focus on how to actually conduct and use it as a model for participants to do the same for their direct reports down the line.

THE RAPID, HIGH-ENGAGEMENT, ALL-EMPLOYEE CASCADE™

Executives, particularly those launching and leading corporate transformations, must learn how to simply focus the organization so that employees can quickly align. They must find new ways to engage employees so that they can lead the organization in new directions at all levels. Moreover, the increasing speed of change and disruption, in general, is forcing the need to engage and align all employees rapidly.

Such trends cause us to bolt an employee supercharger onto the traditionally management-focused process for leading a corporate transformation. The supercharger is the *Rapid, High-engagement, All-employee Cascade™*. We know, a mouthful! But every element of the term is critical to its success.

This unique kind of Cascade must roll out in the organization *rapidly* because employees live in a dynamic world full of distractions. Often, they are skeptical that senior management will hold the course, so movement quickly to early results helps keep energy and commitment high. Moreover, it greatly undermines unified effort if important parts of the organization must wait too long after others have already gone through the transformation engagement process. Indeed, I once worked on a corporate transformation in which a three-person team of corporate HR professionals was sent out to deliver a four-day Cascade program, loaded with lots of employee training and HR policy modules in addition to the essential elements of the transformation game plan and associated commitment setting activities, to 100,000 employees around the world. When they returned to their regular jobs in the corporate headquarters two years later, their work had been lapped by another wave of new corporate strategies!

There are many other reasons why the Cascade rollout needs to be fast. If you dither, don't assume that your competitors are sitting on their hands. And don't wait until you have arrived at the perfect transformation game plan. Move into engagement and execution as soon as possible so that you can begin to harvest the learnings from doing and make refinements in a timely manner. This is especially important in transformation efforts that involve sailing out into uncharted waters.

The Cascade must be designed to elicit *high engagement*. No hyperbolic communication events or employee barbeques are going to get the job done. You must carefully construct and orchestrate occasions that are based on the high-engagement and "safe passage" principles that were discussed in Chapter 5.

And they must involve and engage *all employees*. Successful transformations are all-hands affairs. It is insufficient to anoint the top few levels of leaders with the essence of the corporate transformation game plan, have them delegate the expectations to those below, and hope for the best at the end of the performance year.

This employee-focused, leader-led process needs to be introduced right after the corporate transformation game plan has been developed and the top three levels of leaders have set their commitments to action. As Exhibit 8.2 shows, for maximum employee commitment, the Cascade approach must not only be leader-led, but its reach must far exceed the traditional communications and training approaches that have traditionally been used to introduce change agendas into an organization.

Let's use a NASCAR-based metaphor to illustrate the transition that needs to take place from planning to employee engagement, alignment, and commitment as a corporate transformation unfolds.[6]

The Transformation Engine

Before introducing the employee supercharger, let's briefly review what management must do to build the corporate transformation engine. As we so far have discussed, the up-front role of management in launching a corporate transformation involves confronting reality; developing a new Purpose, Strategic vision, and Success Model; and translating that model into a limited set of balanced Transformation Initiatives that are targeted for quantum improvement in one or two years.

The trick is to narrow the focus of transformation down to a few organization-wide initiatives, no more than three or four, that are targeted for quantum – not incremental – change in a short period of time. Such initiatives usually are made up of a mixture of business goals (performance outcomes) and cultural elements (organizational and people enablers).

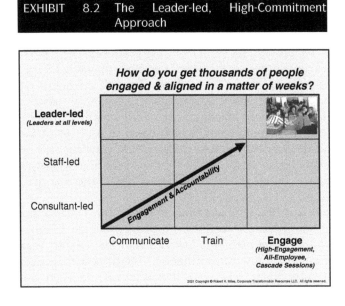

EXHIBIT 8.2 The Leader-led, High-Commitment Approach

How do you get thousands of people engaged & aligned in a matter of weeks?

Leader-led *(Leaders at all levels)*

Staff-led

Consultant-led

Engagement & Accountability

Communicate   Train   **Engage** *(High-Engagement, All-Employee, Cascade Sessions)*

In addition to focusing the enterprise for quantum change, we have shown that management must articulate the set of values or principles that people in the organization will aspire to live by, to guide effective decision-making and aligned behavior in the envisioned new organization. The process of reinforcing the new values and behaviors is often referred to as the culture change required to achieve the desired business and organizational transformation.

Once this limited set of constructs has been developed and agreed upon by top management and appropriately vetted with other important constituencies, the transformation engine has been built. This is what I have been referring to as "sharpening the strategic arrow before putting all the wood behind it." With the key corporate transformation constructs refined and vetted; the major transformation initiatives translated into areas of focus, outcome metrics, and action programs; and the key supporting values anchored in specific, observable behaviors, management has done its job of articulating the desired future state of the enterprise. The block of the transformation engine has been wrought.

Now is the time to bolt on the employee supercharger.

The Employee Supercharger

Leaders supercharge the launch of well-articulated plans for corporate transformation by rapidly and intensively involving *all* employees in high-engagement Cascades that create understanding, dialogue, feedback, and accountability. These Cascades empower people to creatively align their subunits, teams, and individual jobs with the major transformation initiatives of the whole enterprise. If done well, the Cascade events may accomplish their primary mission of refocusing and re-energizing managers and employees by creating an intensive initial experience that can be accomplished in as little as one to one-and-a-half days. The real management challenge is recognizing that they must make such a commitment if they ever hope to engage employees in the contributions they can make to the transformation effort.

What goes on inside a rapid, high-engagement, all-employee Cascade?

First, consider a large room filled with all the managers of a major subunit of a corporation. (A similar setting is subsequently created in which all individual contributors in a subunit join their managers for a one-day, all-employee Cascade event and so on down through the organizational ranks, ending with all individual contributors.) Everyone is assembled around round tables of six to eight managers each. Every manager has his or her own "playbook" for the coming year, which contains a series of modules organized around the key corporate transformation constructs: a review of realities, an articulation of purpose and strategic vision, new success model, the transformation initiatives (one module at a time), and the company values and expected behavior changes.

The kickoff of the Cascade stage is set by the Transformation Leader, who explains the business realities, purpose, strategic vision, and success model and value. Then members of the Senior Leadership Team, who also serve as champions of the transformation initiatives, introduce all managers (and in the subsequent sessions, all employees) to each transformation initiative, as well as to the aligned company values, using a high-engagement methodology.

Tablework teams are created to enable all managers of a subunit to learn about the purpose and strategic vision, as well as the areas of focus and outcome metrics for each transformation initiative before spending time in a dialogue to translate these constructs for meaning and action for their teams and for their own jobs. At the conclusion of each dialogue module, the tablework teams report out their preliminary initiatives and job-level commitments and learn about those of other teams. Then the tablework teams reconvene to discuss what they have learned. They conclude by drafting a near-final set of team or job-level commitments to enable them to align their job behaviors with the initiative. The process is repeated until all three or four transformation initiatives have been translated for job-level action.

To complete the Cascade process, managers in a subunit conduct a subsequent one-day Cascade meeting with all their individual contributors to delineate job-level commitments that have a clear line of sight back to the handful of organization-wide transformation initiatives, as shown in Exhibit 8.3. Employees finalize such individual business commitments with their supervisors during the following two weeks.

The following two figures are provided to give you a tactical feel for how these compressed Cascade sessions are set up for a one-day format, which is typical for the top several levels in an organization. Exhibit 8.4 provides an overview of the Cascade macro agenda. The corporate transformation playbook that all attendees are given contains all the transformation presentations, tablework templates for structured dialogue, and commitment recording forms for quick access. Note that the meeting format is quite compressed to make the best use of participants' time away from work, and simple, structured worksheets are provided to keep discussions on track and everyone focused on the task. (Computers and cell phones are banished from the session unless they have been specifically integrated into the Cascade agenda.)

Multiple departmental teams at the same organizational level usually are assembled with their supervisors around round tables in a large meeting room for this compressed exercise of learning, dialoguing, and commitment setting. The energy in the room is palpable. The sound of an active beehive comes to mind. Not surprising, the toolkit provided to Cascade leaders through one of our clients explained, "The agenda of this one-day Cascade event was designed to be ambitious and to provide a sense of urgency to the transformation process."

As has been observed throughout the book, an essential bias in successful rapid transformations is to get everyone in the pool first, with the knowledge that they're going to be headed toward the deep end, before providing all the training and development needed to make the full traverse of the pool. That is to say, our strong recommendation is to first engage and start the process of learning from executing and then to follow up quickly with training if needed, but not the other way around. With aligned and committed employees in the pool, they will be much more motivated to accept opportunities to learn and develop. Another accelerator of transformations.

Finally, Exhibit 8.5 reveals how the typical values and transformation initiative modules are designed in the rapid, high-engagement Cascade meetings.

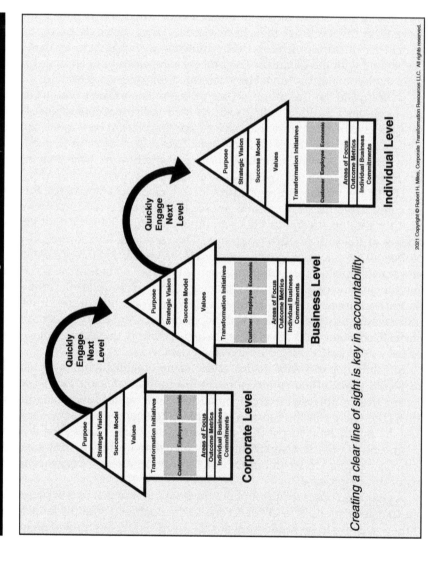

EXHIBIT 8.4   Cascade Macro Agenda

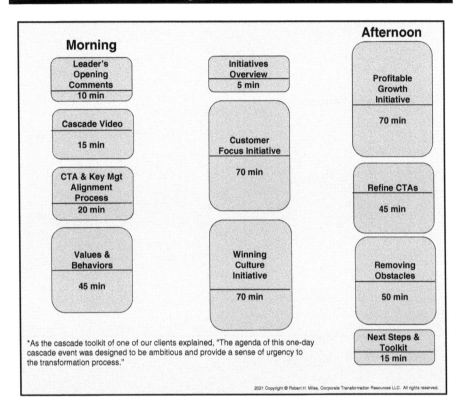

*As the cascade toolkit of one of our clients explained, "The agenda of this one-day cascade event was designed to be ambitious and provide a sense of urgency to the transformation process."

Given the compressed format, the clarity and simplicity of the corporate transformation game plan are essential to Cascade's success. It must be simple enough to easily be translated into job-relevant commitments to action by people and teams at every organization level.

At this juncture, the executive and business leaders have set the transformation game plan, and managers and employees at all levels have gone through a compressed cycle of understanding, dialogue, feedback, alignment, and commitment setting. The accelerated process enables people to use their creativity and job knowledge to take prudent risks at their own job levels to drive the transformation challenge.

How the Employee Supercharger Works

The recent experience of a Silicon Valley-based high-tech firm with 5,000 employees and global operations provides a constructive example of how a Rapid, High-engagement, All-employee Cascade™ works. After top management had spent several months defining where the company needed to go and restructuring it into 14 major subunits, they were able to quickly achieve both subunit alignment and employee engagement by dropping the

EXHIBIT 8.5   Sample Cascade Modules (One-day Format)

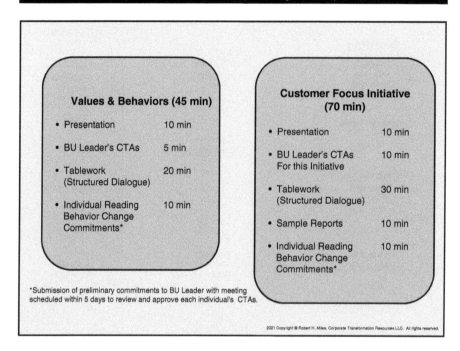

new direction and key initiatives down through the new business and functional subunits.

The chosen vehicle was a multiday Cascade event in each subunit, which involved all its employees and was kicked off by the CEO and then passed to the new subunit leader and management team. All managers in a subunit, say the European Sales organization, were brought on "board during the first two days. They were intensively exposed to the new strategic vision, the core transformation initiatives, and the values and expected behaviors in the intended culture for the corporation and for their own organization. Then all employees in the organization joined in the last two days of the event. At the end of the subunit's four-day, back-to-back, all-manager and all-employee Cascades, a clear line of sight had been created from the new corporate goals, through the goals of the subunit, down to the job-level objectives of all employees in the subunit. A series of similar events took place in rapid succession in all corporate subunits around the globe. The entire high-engagement process was completed in 13 weeks, including a pilot and a "sweeper" event at the end to catch any employees who had not been in the company to attend their subunit's Cascade. Then all the Cascade content was transferred to the new-hire orientation program.

The learning from this 13-week global Cascade has led to greater speed and intensity in the Cascade process in subsequent transformation launches at other corporations. For example, for the 16,000 employees in a global professional services company, the all-managers events were streamlined to one-and-a-half days, and the all-employee Cascade events were reduced to a single day each. The entire Cascade process took only six weeks to complete with a nationally dispersed workforce. A similar streamlined process was implemented at a 600-employee fiber optics switch maker in an organization-wide total of three days.

Source: Robert H. Miles, "Beyond the Age of Dilbert: Accelerating Corporate Transformations by Rapidly Engaging All Employees," Organizational Dynamics, 2001, Vol. 29, No. 4, pp. 313–321. Reprinted by permission.

The Leader-led Double Loop

Consistent with the principles laid out earlier in this chapter, it is critical that the Cascade be leader-led, not led by internal staff professionals or consultants. Because the general, high-engagement format utilizing tablework modules is the same down through the levels, although more streamlined as job scope narrows, a subordinate who goes through a Cascade with his supervisor is fully qualified and equipped when provided a Cascade toolkit, to conduct his own high-engagement Cascade meeting at the next level with his direct reports, and so on. This double looping of activity of leaders at all levels is illustrated in Exhibit 8.6. Without this double-loop feature, a Cascade would not be able to achieve the consistent messaging and high levels of employee engagement, alignment, and commitment to be able to achieve a breakthrough on the transformation initiatives in a short period of time – the hallmark of successful corporate transformations. When a leader at any level

EXHIBIT 8.6   Double Loop in Cascade Rollout at Global Technology Company

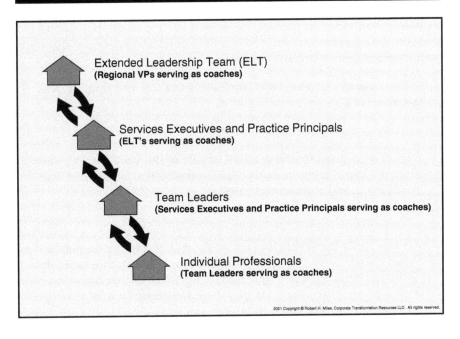

participates in a dialogue with his or her boss and peers and makes commitments, there is a good baseline of alignment and engagement. When that same leader has to stand up and guide his or her own team through an identical Cascade meeting, he or she becomes an evangelist.

> NOTE: A video of the *Rapid, High-engagement, All-employee Cascade*™ in action at a global retailer may be accessed in an my online course, Robert H. Miles, Transformation Leader's Guide: The Online Course, which is discussed at the end of this book.

By having such simultaneous Cascade sessions in a large room, it is possible to deliver the same messages about the components of the Transformation Arrow, keep all supervisor-led sessions on the same schedule, and even have a sampling of tablework report outs in the open forum to help everyone see how their commitments fit into the whole.

EMPLOYEE RESPONSES TO HIGH ENGAGEMENT IN TRANSFORMATION

The responses of employees to the high-engagement Cascade have always been quite favorable. But employees almost always go into their Cascade events with a healthy mixture of confusion, skepticism, and even cynicism. They expect to witness once again a parade of half-baked ideas from an executive team that is not itself in alignment and that has not taken the time to be clear about what is needed and why or to become committed and accountable for following through for execution. Instead, managers and employees at all levels tend to leave the high-engagement Cascade with a very different impression of management and their level of commitment to the corporate transformation process. Here are a few representative quotes from managers and employees who recently had such an experience during the transformation launch in their company:

> "The Cascade process was nothing short of amazing. It was phenomenal."

***

> "I was astounded by the positive impact of the Cascade. We said the very same thing to every single person. It was aligning and motivating, and it produced results."

***

> "It was really incredible. In fact, at the end of the day on Sunday when people were told they only had one task left, they actually groaned! It pulled sales and marketing together like they have never been. Then they wanted to know from me how soon manufacturing was going to go through it."

*****

"It worked. People got the vision, mission, and values. They got to absorb them and tie them to their own jobs."

*****

"It was superb. It was very fast. It was for everybody in the organization. It was focused on a few key things. The focus on 'translation' to relevance for people's own jobs was a key thing in the Cascades."

*****

"Cascades will remain at the highpoint of their careers for many employees many years later in their careers. Open communication. Minimal hierarchy. Very inspirational."

*****

"It was great. It was very well orchestrated. People really worked hard to make it successful. The leaders stepped up to the plate. People left floating on air."

Follow-through on Execution and Learning

Once the corporate transformation table is set and a clear line of sight connecting organization-level transformation initiatives with the job-level performance, and behavior change commitments of all managers and employees have been established, the whole effort is knitted together by the creation of a learning organization in which early failures and successes may be quickly analyzed and shared with all parts of the organization.

Skill or competency deficiencies can now be engaged more fully in the context of a focused, accountable, and truly motivated system. Employees may now seek out training and other competency-enhancing opportunities to be able to meet their new performance commitments. The organization refreshes the entire accelerated transformation process on a quarterly basis by maintaining the ACT process architecture, which consists of the Transformation Leader and his or her executive team, the normal line and staff management structure, transformation initiative co-champions, the Process Support Team, a quarterly cycle of leadership follow-through meetings and mini-cascades, and occasional focus groups that tap various parts and levels of the enterprise. We will cover these important elements of the transformation process architecture in the next chapter, which focuses on the Execute Phase.

Cascade as Transformation "Accelerator"

Given the repeated successes across a variety of service, manufacturing, and high-technology organizations of the *Rapid, High-engagement, All-employee Cascade*™, a few fundamental reflections may be drawn. Such an intervention at the end of the initial corporate transformation-planning phase has the very definite effect of *accelerating* the entire corporate transformation process. It quickly *aligns* the entire company around a limited set of important transformation constructs: purpose, strategic vision, success model, values, and transformation initiatives. It *engages* everyone at or near the moment of transformation launch, enabling them through a process of structured dialogue to use their untapped creativity to redefine the way they behave and perform at work to uniquely support the transformation effort. It does so *rapidly*.

Cascade as Leadership and Organization Development

The *Rapid, High-engagement, All-employee Cascade*™ also serves as a powerful, experiential intervention for developing leaders at all levels in the organization. Not only does such a Cascade empower employees to take initiative at their level and help launch the repositioning or revitalization of an enterprise, but it also serves as a fundamental "Leadership 101" intervention for everyone in the organization. Indeed, within the one to one-and-a-half-day Cascade event, everyone learns how to effectively confront reality, develop a compelling purpose, strategic vision, and success model, articulate a new set of values and behaviors to guide decision-making, and distill a limited set of transformation initiatives to focus the entire organization. In addition, everyone learns how to communicate these constructs in a simple and compelling manner, engage people in structured dialogue, facilitate constructive feedback and establish personal accountability for the new performance expectations.

What follows the actual Cascade event is a demonstration throughout the remainder of the year about what it means to follow through to ensure execution and to create a learning organization to get better at the things that were right at Launch and to make modifications for improvement in those that don't measure up. Indeed, the whole process of refocusing the organization and re-engaging all employees is repeated in a more streamlined manner to launch the second and each successive year of the corporate transformation effort, thereby working these leadership expectations and competencies deeply into the marrow of the enterprise's management process.

Overcoming the "Buts"

Despite all of the positive contributions of the *Rapid, High-engagement, All-employee Cascade*™, leaders operating under outmoded notions of the organization-individual relationship can usually conjure up a long enough list of potential caveats to dampen the enthusiasm of all but the hardiest Transformation Leaders. Among the initial protestations are the following list of favorite fears:

- Managers don't have enough time
- The organization doesn't have sufficient process skills to pull it off
- We can't afford to have everyone away from their jobs at the same time
- We need to get everything right before we launch
- You can't just drop employees into one of these without getting them ready first
- It's too much of a hardship for people to travel to remote Cascade settings

The act of moving beyond such protestations – the process of "overcoming the buts" – falls squarely on the Transformation Leader.

All it takes is for the Transformation Leader to turn the problem back for creative resolution. For example, executives planning the Cascade of a 500-strong, US-based customer service support department were initially perplexed about how to keep customers satisfied while abandoning the phones to attend their Cascade event. They were told by the CEO to come back with a plan. The response was to inform customers well in advance about the event and its role in enhancing customer service, to have the managers' portion of the Cascade event over the weekend, to augment the services staff the week before and after the Cascade to handle overloads, to bring in skeleton customer services staffers from Asia and Europe to minimally cover the situation, and to have services managers on call from the Cascade site the second two days when their employees were going through the process.

Even though there will usually be challenges like this to the use of high-engagement approaches, a creative leadership team can almost always find a way to move ahead. And the payoffs during transformation launches, which often stall during or shortly after lift-off, are tremendous.

It demands that executive leaders use all their creativity to engage employees in more fundamental ways that help them more quickly understand and align with the ongoing process of corporate transformation.

The simultaneous challenges of high employee value and high rates of required change make it absolutely essential that executive leaders develop more accelerated approaches to corporate transformation and more intensive methodologies for engaging, aligning, and motivating all employees; indeed, for creating Transformation Leaders at all levels in the enterprise.

TIPS FOR ENGAGEMENT

- Build the capability to engage in dialogue through a tightly structured *Rapid, High-engagement, All-employee Cascade*™ process that is leader-led.
- Expect top-to-bottom engagement in a matter of weeks, even for teams of 10,000+ employees, by leveraging the different management levels.
- Keep each level of management in direct dialogue with their teams – don't just rely on communicating broadly to the masses to get the message across. Indeed, be sure to keep the organization's Communications function tightly aligned to the transformation constructs and process.
- Keep engagement focused on the top corporate priorities (for example, purpose, strategic vision, success model, transformation initiatives, supporting areas of focus, and values).

Notes

1. Portions of this chapter were adapted from Robert H. Miles, "Accelerating Corporate Transformations: Don't Lose Your Nerve!, Harvard Business Review," January-February 2010; Robert H. Miles and Michael Kanazwa, Big Ideas to Big Results: Leading Corporate Transformation in a Disruptive Word (Pearson, Second Edition), 2016; and Robert H. Miles, "Beyond the Age of Dilbert: Accelerating Corporate

Transformations by Engaging All Employees," Organization Dynamics, Special Edition, Summer 2001.

2. Survey by Harris Interactive of 11,045 workers.

3. Kenexa, a Wayne-based provider of solutions for employee hiring and retention. The survey compiles more than 840,000 responses from U.S. and U.K. multinational companies. "Usually, employees hit bottom in the three- to five-year range," said Jeffrey Saltzman, Kenexa's New York practice leader, who helped organize the survey.

4. Robert H. Miles, "Type I Transformation: Repositioning America's Most Admired Utility," Chapter 5, Leading Corporate Transformations: Blueprint for Business Renewal, San Francisco: Jossey-Bass Publishers, A Division of John Wiley & Sons, 1997, p. 123.

5. A term coined by Jim Nassikas, who turned around the venerable Stanford Court Hotel atop Nob Hill in San Francisco before developing the award-winning Deer Valley Resort in Park City, Utah.

6. For more detailed case studies of the deployment of the Rapid, High-engagement, All-employee Cascade, refer to Robert H. Miles, Leading Corporate Transformation: Blueprint for Business Renewal, San Francisco: Jossey-Bass Publishers, a division of John Wiley & Sons, 1997.

CHAPTER 9

The Execute Phase

"A successful launch only puts a leader at the starting gate of transformation."

OVER THE HUMP AND INTO THE SLUMP[1]

Jubilation was in the air shortly after the transformation effort at one telecommunications giant began. The CEO was so thrilled with the problem-plagued company's early-stage success in confronting reality and getting people thinking and acting differently that he began to talk about it in public appearances and in interviews with *Forbes* and the *Wall Street Journal*. There's nothing wrong with savoring little victories, but this leader also began to disengage ever so slightly from his involvement with the transformation process.

Soon, an attitude of "Hey, we're over the hump" crept through the entire company; the intensity and sense of urgency that marked the beginning of the transformation process began to wane. Here was a company entering one of the most competitive periods in its history, and people were lapsing back into a business-as-usual state. The old guard political structures came to life again, and agents of change lost the support and protection they needed to shepherd the transformation through the remaining minefields of execution. The company might have been over the hump, but now it was into the slump. The transformation never got back on track and, eventually, the company was taken over by a larger, more agile competitor.

Or consider how another company slid into the slump from what seemed like a safe perch. A couple of years into the transformation process, this organization had broken out of a flat-to-shrinking growth trend. They had successfully shifted from being a company that grew through acquisitions to one that only drove growth internally through innovations from customer-focused business units. The company saw whole new arenas of opportunity on the horizon. With the top leadership and employees at every level fully engaged, the rewards were beginning to flow.

Although they could have doubled down on their bets, they began to hedge and make smaller bets instead. They began to compete by simply putting out revisions of products with a few more features rather than challenging the market with new categories of products or new business

DOI: 10.4324/9781003272724-9

success models. It was a time when the team could have stretched even further than was possible in the first and second years, but instead, the team fell back into cautious, incremental decision-making. The slump was under way, proving the maxim that the better the process goes up front, the bigger the risk for a slump.

Following a great transformation Launch is tough. How can you keep your people energized and focused? As the natural tendency to slump takes root, leaders often look for the next "big thing" to bring the energy back up. At times, they have looked at the ACT process as a planning and launch vehicle, and once the plan is announced and performance management is reset at the front end of the Execute Phase, they are keen to pursue new issues and strategic ideas. So, shortly after the Cascade Phase, they drift into adding new programs. They ignore the absolutely critical Execute and Replanning Phases of an ACT-based transformation. But by doing this, they put their organizations right back into the clutches of Gridlock. The system gets overloaded with yet more initiatives and people see another flavor-of-the-day program in their rearview mirror. They drift back to the old ways of operating, and progress grinds to a snail's pace.

You can't completely avoid the execution "slumps." The best way to minimize them is to anticipate when they will emerge and design specific interventions at these predictable waypoints into your transformation roadmap to handle them. The execution inhibitors and accelerators were briefly introduced in Chapters 1 and 2. In this chapter, I want to delve more deeply into the dynamics of this group of inhibitors and show how ACT is uniquely designed to help you confront and overcome the execution humps and slumps.[2]

As a refresher, the three predictable slumps during the Execute Phase tend to take place as follows:

- *Post-Launch* – The first quarterly checkpoint after a full and intensive Launch Phase, right after the Cascade has been completed
- *Midcourse* – The third quarter going into a final push for year-end results
- *Relaunch* – The re-planning and relaunch of the next performance year

Hump #1: The Post-Launch Blues

Gearing up a full organization for a strategic pivot or big boost in growth is absolutely hard work. Doing it in a three- to four-month cycle is an all-out sprint. If the organization hasn't been used to speed and high engagement, this can be exhausting.

Some members of the team will want to sally forth. But others may feel a strong urge to sit back following the intensive Launch and Cascade Phases to take a breather. This execution hump is the *Post-Launch Blues*. As one executive in an ACT-based project explained:

> *It is like you've just run a 400-meter, full-out sprint. As you cross what you think is the finish line, you're told, great first lap, but you're actually running a marathon. So, good start, but keep up the pace!*

This reaction is normal and expected. After the Cascade work sessions are complete throughout the organization and every person has developed line-of-sight individual *Commitments to Action (CTAs)*, people really do need to get down to the business of executing what they said they would do. This requires more tactical focus and energy. Sometimes this shift in focus from planning to doing is mistaken as a departure from the new emphases in high engagement and breakthrough thinking back to the "old way" of doing things. And in some cases, that is what happens.

As the day-to-day pressure and grind retake center stage during the first quarter into the Execute Phase, old habits can gradually sneak up on the system. Leaders who were working in a more open and engaging mode can switch back to the command-and-control mode. And priorities set in the Launch Phase will be challenged as immediate expense pressures arise and revenue and other tactical goals must be met. Recall the definition of transformation articulated earlier as "A few well-articulated initiatives targeted for breakthrough results in a short period of time ... in a sea of necessary incremental improvements."

At the same time, as the Transformation Leader, you might begin to feel as though you've done your part in getting the process in gear. Because the full roadmap, strategic direction, and transformation initiatives have been launched and cascaded, you may feel that it is now time for the team to simply execute.

But delegation cannot be given over to abdication. With delegation, the leader must stay firmly engaged. He or she cannot allow the important incremental to-dos swamp the transformation game plan. He or she must actively champion the Transformation Initiatives and visibly model the new desired behaviors. It will not be sufficient for leaders to simply endorse or preside over these things. There is a saying about the messages of leaders that goes something like, "Just when you are sick of saying it, they are just beginning to hear it."

Ballast and Keel

There is an important dimension of leadership that is quite boring to many creative, hard-charging types. It is serving as the ballast and keel for the company. The concept was briefly covered in Chapter 2. Ballast is the weight that keeps a ship upright when the winds, waves, or other external conditions try to tip it over, and the keel is used to hold the ship on a straight course. This role of holding the course and keeping things grounded sounds different from the role of a Transformational Leader, whose job is to take the company to new heights and get people to break out of old patterns.

Coming off of a high at the end of the Launch Phase, at which the leadership team is energized, focused, and engaged can be confusing for the leader, who must switch into the ballast-and-keel role. However, that is just what is needed following a strong Launch. The Transformation Leader must set the stage for all the leaders, managers, and supervisors down below. Starting at the top, each of them must kick off their weekly staff meetings during the Execute Phase with a review of the transformation initiatives progress, call attention to people and plans that have drifted out of alignment, and communicate the same message over and over. Only then will it be visible to all that their leader has effectively shifted into an execution mode.

All the normal communications channels need to feather into this flow as well. A forewarning to creative Corporate Communications people in the organization: You too will sometimes find it hard to hammer the same message repeatedly rather than put out fresh content at each new opportunity. You too need to follow the ballast-and-keel analogy if the organization is to stay on the transformation track.

The half-life for many corporate transformation programs is just about a quarter or two during the Execute Phase. People throughout the organization will be watching to see if this effort has been just another flavor of the month. It's up to you to make sure your transformation game plan remains on the track you and your team have so carefully laid.

Company-Wide Transformation Initiative Teams

In addition to the conviction and commitment of the leaders to the plan, there is a need, especially in the early stages, to make sure that the transformation initiatives are fully sponsored and driven from the top. The key to building traction with the initiatives is to make sure that they are orchestrated from both performance and learning perspectives. On the performance side, they must become a part of the normal daily running of the business rather than be treated as a special program or overlay. On the learning side, there has to be execution "oversight." Senior executives need to play both roles. *All members of the Senior Leadership Team (SLT) should serve as companywide Co-Champions of one of the Transformation Initiatives, and each SLT member is responsible for driving all the corporate Transformation Initiatives in his or her part of the organization.*

In ACT parlance, this is the *"Two Hats"* of executive leadership, as shown in Exhibit 9.1.

The structure for doing this starts long before arriving at the Execute Phase, with the creation of the SLT-level Transformation Initiative Team Co-Champions reporting directly to the Transformation Leader at the beginning of the corporate transformation Launch Phase. Their initial job was to bring a cross-functional perspective to the operationalization of their assigned initiative. With the requirement that all SLT members have a role in shaping these initiatives and in vetting them with their peers, the ACT-based setup ensured that all senior corporate leaders were engaged in the transformation and that more than just one functional or business perspective would be influential in shaping each initiative.

For example, charged with developing, say, a "People Initiative," a business unit executive would typically co-chair the effort with the head of Human Resources, and those two would walk their initiative through a series of steps in the ACT process where they would be scrubbed by their peers until approved for rollout during the Cascade and Execute Phases. Moreover, after approval by the Transformation Leader and the SLT peers, each member of the SLT would set Commitments to Action (CTAs), vetted by their peers and approved by the leader, to drive *all* the initiatives in their part of

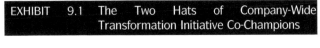

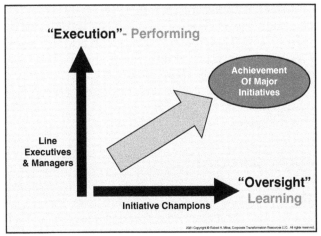

EXHIBIT 9.1 The Two Hats of Company-Wide Transformation Initiative Co-Champions

the organization. This much was reviewed in detail in Chapter 4 "Structuring Your Transformation Launch."

With their experience in building the Transformation Initiatives, the company-wide Co-Champions next bring aboard their Initiative Team's divisional initiative champions for every major component in the organization just prior to the shift into the Execute Phase. These cross-functional teams become responsible for *execution oversight*, which includes the following duties at company and divisional or department levels: (a) measurement progress against metrics on their initiative, (b) identification of emerging gaps or shortfalls in their execution, (c) collection and sharing of leading practices on their Transformation Initiative across the organization, and (d) communication to all employees of needed refinements and course corrections.

Execution "Oversight"

During the Launch Phase, the role of company-wide Transformation Initiative teams is easily understood. Taking a cross-company perspective, it is their job to build and then vet their assigned initiative so that it may be rolled out to the entire enterprise during the Cascade Phase.

However, when these company-wide Initiative Teams transition over to the Execute Phase, some Senior Leadership Team members and their divisional counterparts are initially confused about what the term execution "oversight" means as applied to their role as Co-Champions. What works is to have each set of initiative Co-Champions and their company-wide teams share primary responsibility for overseeing progress on and learning about their assigned transformation initiative during the Execute Phase. This role is quite different from the particular line-management responsibility that each manager has for driving all the initiatives in his or her area of authority. Quite simply, the burden of driving the execution of all the company-wide transformation initiatives should not fall solely on the Initiative Co-Champions. The achievement of these initiatives remains the responsibility of all line and functional managers, who each own in their published CTAs as part of all the actions required for success.

So, to be doubly clear, the execution oversight duties of a company or divisional initiative Co-Champion are assumed in addition to whatever line or functional management responsibilities he or she might have for achieving *all* the corporate-wide Transformation Initiatives based on his or her personal CTAs. None of the other executives and managers are off the hook from having accountability to execute on their part of *all* the corporate Transformation Initiatives.

Quarterly Leadership Checkpoints

The Company-wide Initiative Teams have two primary vehicles for getting their jobs done so that line managers, together with their supervisors and individual contributors throughout the organization, can do their best job of implementing the Transformation Initiatives in their sphere of authority and job scope. One is the quarterly, one-day meeting of the Extended Leadership Team (ELT), the top three levels of management. The other is the Quarterly Mini-Cascade. The Mini-Cascade vehicle is essential for getting timely information to everyone in the company on progress and quick refinements in courses of action to accelerate the execution of the corporate Transformation Initiatives. Each department in the company needs to roll out its own Mini-Cascade immediately following the quarterly ELT checkpoint event. We will come back to this ACT-based execution element later in the chapter.

The quarterly ELT checkpoint meeting consists of the Transformation Leader, his or her direct reports, and their direct reports; a convening of all of the business and functional departments in the company. The company-wide initiative team Co-Champions share progress of their initiative, as well as lessons learned throughout the enterprise and needed refinements, in a carefully structured and simple format. It should be no surprise that the department teams are organized around tables together so that with their SLT leader, they can use tablework and structured dialogue to make sense of what they hear about each initiative, translate, and prioritize that information for relevance, and develop a plan for informing and reengaging all members of their organization with the rollout of their own quarterly Mini-Cascade.

The way in which each company-wide initiative team prepares for this quarterly checkpoint event led by the Transformation Leader is summarized in Exhibit 9.2.

With a well-structured quarterly checkpoint that tests progress and accountability and that reengages the team, new life will be driven into the execution of next quarter's performance. This renews the faith that management will follow through, builds confidence that everyone is headed down the right path, and reinforces the sense that accountability for the CTAs is real. This becomes the fuel that will drive the transformation forward long after the excitement of Launch.

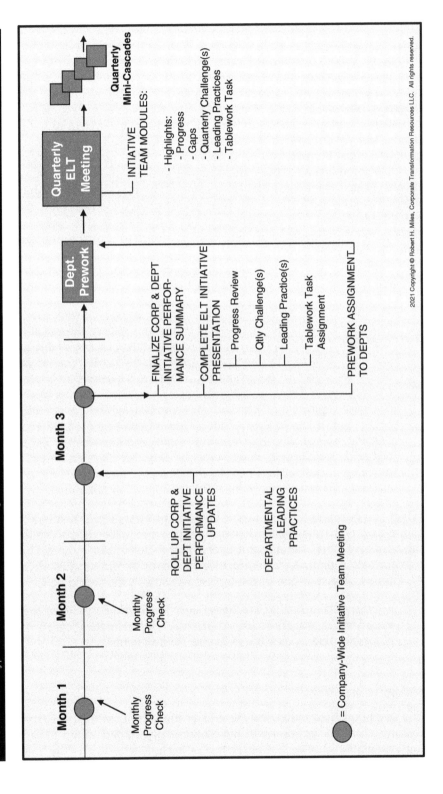

EXHIBIT 9.2 Typical Initiative Team Meeting Schedule: Driving Execution

Hump #2: Midcourse Overconfidence

The next high-risk point for a major execution slump typically comes after two quarterly checkpoints or so have passed. Now, at about six to eight months following the Launch, results are starting to build momentum. The process itself is very well understood and is being used in many parts of the organization. To return to the sailing analogy, land is dropping out of sight over the transom of the launch vehicle, and a feeling of smooth sailing without need of course corrections can set in. Employees have survived the new language system of the transformation and have mastered its methodology. They ease back into the captain's chair and begin to relax. You have reached the *Midcourse Overconfidence* hump.

During this part of the transformation process, there will most certainly be unexpected challenges that have come up along the way and things that aren't working perfectly with your transformation game plan. Such inevitable challenges and issues become opportunities for those who want out from under the accountability and rigor or desire to return to the "good old days" to take their shot.

Sometimes after the second quarterly checkpoint, you'll get a comment or email message that looks something like this:

> *Well, this process has really worked well so far overall, but I think we've gotten the best out of it that we can at this point. The work sessions at the last quarterly checkpoint weren't really as creative as before, and people just don't need to keep having dialogues and tablework. We were just talking about tactical things anyway. Wasn't this supposed to be about transformation? What we really need now to move the business forward is a hit of innovation to break out our performance. Next quarter might be the right time to have an off-site on innovation using a new break-set thinking method I've been reading about. We can shorten up the tablework activities to make room for this. All that discussion is becoming a waste of time anyway. I'll be happy to coordinate the next quarterly checkpoint and really kick it up a notch on innovation.*

When you get a request like this, if you don't step up right then to affirm the commitments that have been so carefully put into place, others can derail all the hard work that initially got everything focused and moving down the transformation path. As a Senior Vice President of Human Resources in an ACT-based project at one of the largest retailers in the world observed:

> *Transformations have to be a "never-done" approach. People want to see an end to it so they can go back to "normal." But really living the process of transforming is what has to become the new normal.*

Midcourse Assessment

The key point here is that by the end of the second to third quarter of the Execute Phase the process will have necessarily shifted into a more tactical implementation mode; that is what it is designed to do. As the "newness" and excitement of the transformation launch wear off, some people can be expected to start suggesting new methods that are more to their liking and better aligned with their existing skills. Listen for the real process refinements that are needed and act on them without delay. But make sure you have established a process for gathering midcourse inputs from everyone; not just the vocal few.

Because of this predictable pattern, the final quarterly checkpoint of the year – the one at the end of the third quarter – is the perfect point to have a rigorous, multilevel, midcourse assessment of the process itself and transformation progress overall. The idea of the midcourse assessment is to channel any frustrations or shortcomings with the process toward improvements for next year's process. It will always be the case that the transformation process doesn't work perfectly the first time through and that it will take some time and practice for it to meld into the way the business is run – the core management process. For that reason, it is important to conduct a deep-dive assessment of the transformation process itself, with no stones unturned and no levels skipped, to obtain firsthand feedback about what's working and what needs to be changed in all jobs and at all levels. Usually, this internal assessment involves everyone on the leadership team (the Transformation Leader and the SLT and ELT), as well as samplings at the manager and supervisor levels, and cross-functional focus group discussions at the employee level.

A sample of the Midcourse Assessment interview protocol for the top three levels of executives is included in Appendix 3.

Quarterly Mini-Cascades

There are many subtle but powerful sources of traction that are available to help a leader sustain forward momentum and guard against the occurrence of a slump.

Beyond the rigorous Midcourse Assessment, the quarterly Leadership Checkpoints, and the active championing by the Transformation Leader, and company-wide Initiative Co-Champions and their teams, there are other ways to help increase traction during transformation midcourse. One that works particularly well is a complement to the quarterly checkpoint meetings of the ELT. You can think of this intervention as the Mini-Cascade, and it takes place at *all* levels of the company on a quarterly basis.

The quarterly Mini-Cascade, which takes the form of a streamlined version of the initial *Rapid, High-Engagement, All-Employee Cascade*™, immediately follows each quarterly ELT checkpoint meeting. The Cascade and Mini-Cascades are marked by the same process of sharing a common view of market and business performance realities, restating the direction, and spending time in working sessions to translate the higher-level plans into refined local actions and accountabilities.

Before you jump to the conclusion that these steps might be overkill, consider how simple these powerful interventions actually are. Mini-Cascades are a big deal in maintaining momentum, but they don't have to be treated as expensive, time-consuming, over-produced events. In fact, the more the Mini-Cascades are simply a part of daily operations, the better. Some of the most successful quarterly Mini-Cascades have been ones that store managers have organized with their sales personnel around a pot of coffee and a box of donuts for two hours before the doors open to customers.

Regardless of how simple the setting you choose for quarterly Mini-Cascades, the important thing is that they keep everyone, not just the executives at the top, engaged and informed. They bring to everyone in the organization a candid assessment of progress, news about best practices that have been identified during execution, and carefully selected challenges to help accelerate progress at all levels in the company.

By refreshing the entire organization in this simple manner on a continuing basis during the Execute Phase, you also maintain the clear line of sight from top to bottom in the organization that you created with the initial Cascade during the Launch Phase. This makes it easy to spot intermediate leaders between you and the rest of the organization who are actively driving and those who are blocking the forward movement of the effort. In essence, by sticking with the Mini-Cascades each quarter, you continue to reinforce the critical elements of alignment and accountability at all levels. This empowers engaged employees lower in the organization to exert upward pressure to help sustain the alignment of the supervisors, which complements and reinforces what you are driving from above.

The key to making the Mini-Cascades work is in keeping them simple and focused on conversations with supervisors and their teams at all levels. For example, one company was looking to drive accountability to individual commitments on an ongoing basis. For this, they leveraged technology that would allow managers and employees to use a standard Web-based tool to set and track performance. They believed that would give managers an easy way to have ongoing check-ins on performance. But compliance was considered having 100% of your employees' goals input into the system, not necessarily the quality of the goals. As a result, compliance was above 90%, but the goals were not well thought out, and many managers just demanded that people input their goals. They never had an actual conversation with the person either up front or over time. Instead, they relied more on the corporate recording system than on quarterly performance checkpoints at all levels to drive follow-through. Their focus on administrative compliance and on tools rather than meaningful conversations diluted the effectiveness of their follow-through efforts.

In one transforming high-tech company that had gone through an ACT-based Launch Phase, employees kept the focus on the transformation initiatives by embracing the simple concept of declaring their performance commitments as individuals and as teams, starting at the top and going all the way through the organization. During the first quarter after the initial transformation launch, one-page paper forms that showed the individual team members' goals began to be posted in the hallways around their offices. One team, which was proud of the challenges they had taken on, posted their sheets in the hallway around their work area. Then the idea of posting caught on throughout the company. During the quarterly performance checkpoints and Mini-Cascades, the leaders talked about how to accelerate things that were already working and how to course correct things that were lagging. The leaders each updated their personal CTAs to reflect needed changes, often electing not to change the original numerical goals, but to shift their CTAs in order to accelerate performance of the initiatives. Each leader would work with his or her immediate team and then on down through the full organization until all employees had been through the Mini-Cascade. These quarterly meetings were not expensive, time-consuming, or overly produced affairs. They were simply the normal staff meetings and tailgate operations meetings that were happening anyway. However, instead of reviewing new policies and discussing other administrative items, they would use one meeting per quarter to focus on translating transformation initiatives for action at the immediate job level.

Amazingly, employees would update their team and individual commitments, and you'd see a refreshed set of commitments posted in the hallway just a few weeks after the executives reset their priorities and commitments at quarterly ELT Meetings. The resetting at all levels would be in response to challenges and best practices that had been clearly articulated to everyone based on work by the top three levels of leadership at the company's checkpoint meeting. The role modeling of the Extended Leadership Team, the push to make the commitments real, and the continual drive for improvement during the ACT-based Execute Phase are what drove refinements in everyone's on-the-job commitments and performance.

Creating Mini-Cascades that dovetail into the normal operations of the organization is what kept the energy and commitment high enough to avoid any major slumps. When the CTAs were posted on the walls, they became a constant reminder of the transformation priorities. When each level of management took time to hold a quarterly Mini-Cascade, it provided an opportunity for everyone at all levels to reengage, recommit, and refocus, which is something that everyone can use at least on a quarterly basis.

Quarterly performance checkpoints and especially the Mini-Cascades are often events during which you may observe some leaders start to cut corners on the process. You'll need to continually keep the transformation roadmap in front of everyone, as well as some creativity and humor in these events, to keep everyone engaged and focused. Sending out a video from the Transformation Leader immediately informing everyone about the transformation updates from the quarterly leader checkpoint will help a lot too. This direct connection down through the organization level will also help maintain a clear line of sight from top to bottom, as well as keep any supervisors and managers in between from wavering and sending mixed messages.

The ACT-based corporate transformation process that incorporates these elements during the Execute Phase is summarized in Exhibit 9.3. It emphasizes the need for company-wide mini-cascades to immediately roll out after each quarterly checkpoint meeting of the top three levels of management; the same group of SLT and ELT leaders who crafted the transformation game plan during the Launch Phase. The figure also reminds us that in parallel to the continued focus on the major initiatives in the game plan, the leadership team must also keep track of important strategic and

EXHIBIT 9.3 Execute Phase Roadmap

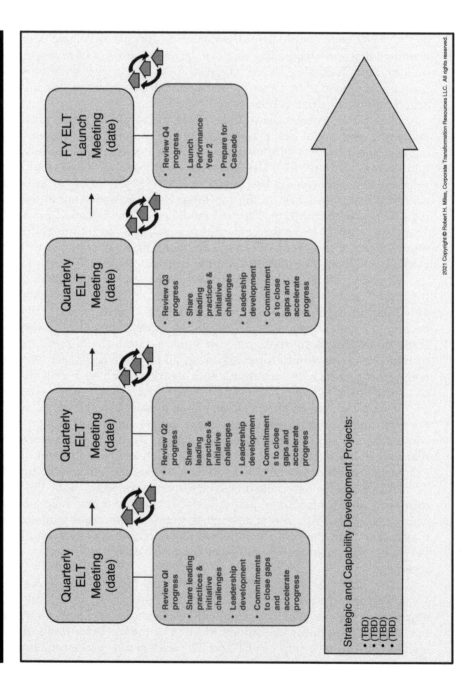

capability projects that were not ready for prime time at the beginning of the Execute Phase, but that may be feathered into the process when they are ready to go.

Hump #3: Presumption of Perpetual Motion

This brings us to the final high-risk hump, the *Presumption of Perpetual Motion*, the observation that first-year success breeds among some executives the belief that "because things are going so well, why do we need to intervene?" This hump rears its head right before the end of the first performance year when everyone is trying to figure out what's next. And you know you have a case of it if one of the members of your leadership team comes up to you and asks, "We don't have to go through that all over again, do we?" You must reply, "Absolutely! Only in a more streamlined fashion with the wisdom gained from year one."

Launching Year 2

The biggest challenge in launching the next performance year, which makes it different from the other two slump points, is the need to confront reality again. But how much of a rethinking of such core transformation constructs as Purpose, Strategic Vision, Success Model, Transformation Initiatives and Company Values do you want to encourage? So much momentum has been built and depth of understanding of the new direction that it would certainly derail progress to scrap everything and start fresh. And it is always hard for the Transformation Leader and the key executives to work up the energy to go through a full re-planning and relaunch cycle. On the other hand, it should also be clear at this point that a lack of regular reality confrontations is exactly what puts most companies behind the eight ball in the first place, so it is always warranted even if difficult.

The key to anticipating and avoiding this slump is to ready the organization for the next full performance year by running it through a complete, more streamlined set of confronting reality, focused alignment, and engagement phases. These are the same phases you employed during the initial launch, only now in a more compressed and informed fashion than the first time around. The baseline customer needs, market, and competitive content and process assessments have already been established. But still, take nothing for granted and challenge everything before you finalize the key initiatives for the next year. Moreover, if you did it right the first time, managers and employees will catch you in the hallways and ask you when they are going to receive their playbook for the next year. They'll actually be looking forward to reengaging and recommitting.

Don't disappoint these enthusiastic allies.

The ACT Method is designed to be repeated on an annual cycle, each year on a more streamlined basis. There is some overlap between years where the current year's plans are being executed and the next year's plans are being created. But the basic re-planning steps of confronting reality, focus, alignment, and engagement need to occur – on an increasingly streamlined basis – for each successive performance year. By repeating the core ACT phases on an annual basis, the ACT principles become part of a more rigorous management and business planning process.

During each annual refresh, run through another round of confidential executive interviews, and don't forget the relevant recommendations you gathered from the Midcourse Assessment. Make sure to talk again with customers, as well as noncustomers, and reassess major competitor and market trends from an outside-in perspective.

With all of that said, there is no reason to automatically scrap all of the existing plans and momentum. It is likely that much of a given year's plans will still be valid for the next year. In fact, many Transformation-level Initiatives will be, by their nature, multiyear efforts. But inevitably, based on performance and learning the prior year, some of the Areas of Focus and the Outcome Metrics that fall within the key corporate Transformation Initiatives will almost certainly need to be refreshed and refocused.

If a Strategic Vision is strong enough, it should provide a constant pull forward by creating a tension between today's reality and where the company is going. If it is still serving this purpose, keep it as is. If the Success Model is still correct and is proving to be a strong competitive advantage, keep it. These elements typically run in longer cycles than a single year.

Transformation Initiatives can run in shorter cycles, especially at the level of the specific Areas of Focus for execution within each initiative. For example, in the case of one retailer, the first-year Transformation Initiatives included Customer Focus, Winning Culture, and Profitable Growth. The initial Customer Focus Initiative was aimed at improving the price/value perception customers had of the company, improving customer experience, and establishing the brand. As they entered the second year, there was a lively debate about the most appropriate Areas of Focus for this Initiative for the next year.

The price/value perception had been a surprise as a big impediment to growth for the company. The initial reality confrontation had revealed that customers believed the company had the worst price/value proposition of their competitive set. This meant that in many cases when customers would make up their comparison-shopping list, the company's stores would not be included. For this reason, the merchandising organization hit this issue hard in the first year by putting major programs in place to shift perception and the realities of their pricing strategies. As a result, the company had closed the competitive gap based on external surveys by the end of the first performance year. Revenue growth and higher margins had been achieved, and the company had its highest single sales day in history in that year. So as the transformation initiatives were being reexamined for the next year, price/value perception as an Area of Focus within the company's Customer Focus Initiative was removed. Most agreed with this decision, but some executives were quite concerned that it would signal a relaxation on the pricing issue. In the end, the executive team declared victory on that Area of Focus and agreed that managing competitive pricing would simply become part of the ongoing operational focus and didn't need special attention.

The other two Areas of Focus within the Customer Focus Initiative now needed more attention. Brand positioning had been firmed up by marketing during the previous year and now needed to be rolled out companywide. The goal was to focus on all customer-facing employees as living examples of the brand itself, which required a full engagement of the organization and focused execution on specifically designing training and programs. Also, the work on developing the customer experience Area of Focus in the first year had concentrated almost exclusively on improving the atmosphere of the stores. A more comprehensive approach would be needed for this Area of Focus in year 2 that would go deeper into product mix, solution positioning for target segments, and more fundamental changes to the shopping environment.

A sharpening of the Strategic Vision in year 2 to focus more on small business customers dictated that the customer experience should also now be more fully targeted across the store and especially with the sales consultants and service technicians to small business customers. So, the two remaining Areas of Focus under the Customer Focus Initiative were tuned up and launched in the second year.

They were given extra attention and resources that would otherwise have been diverted to support the former price/value perception Area of Focus within the Customer Focus Initiative. This example shows how the business initiatives can be reset and stretched at the launch of each new performance year while maintaining the same overall process architecture for the transformation game plan.

No Time to Relax

From the beginning of the Launch through the first full performance year, all leaders are specifically called on to implement a new operating model and launch a major transformation of the business. They are also asked to commit to and personally model needed behavioral changes that are aligned with the new vision and purpose as well as the transformation initiatives. As you approach the front edge of year 2, the values and the behaviors that were pointed out at the beginning of the transformation as critical to driving the change can easily fade into the background if you are not vigilant. By now, transformation traction has begun to settle in and important things are moving forward; many wonder why they need to refresh and relaunch the transformation game plan.

As the leader, you must set the tone for the amount of energy, rigor, and competitiveness that goes into the process of confronting reality from year to year. The more energy and focus you continue to visibly invest that process, the greater the organization will stretch. Given the right process architecture, you will always be in a good position to deftly adjust the amount of stretch you and the members of your team are willing and able to take on each new performance year.

The common theme you might notice across the antidotes for the three slumps is that there is a huge responsibility on the shoulders of Transformation Leaders to set the tone for pressing forward.

Some transformers are often so eager to succeed that they exhaust their energy on the planning and launching stages. They do such a great job of confronting reality, focusing their organizations on the critical areas of transformation, and engaging the executive team in the process that they experience a kind of euphoria that leads them to put the crucial next stage of execution and accountability on cruise control. Some are of the old school in which "Commanders" figure everything out and then toss it all over the fence for the rest to get the job done. They rely on the initial excitement and momentum they created to carry the transformation process through to its conclusion. It doesn't work that way. As the leader, you need to always be on your game and particularly alert to the threat of slump and derailment at the three critical points following the transformation launch.

ACT Overlay Melds into the General Management Process

By building quarter by quarter on previous successes with the transformation process, ACT over time will become indistinguishable from what everyone in the organization comes to view as "our management process." By continually taking on larger challenges using the same, simple, known architecture, your management process will become more streamlined, agile, and stronger. Over time, its sustained focus on the key elements – the new vision and purpose of the company, and its strategy, its unique transformation initiatives and be-havior change commitments, and its widespread use of engagement and structured dialogue, will fundamentally reshape the culture of the enterprise. At that point, you and your team will be able to spend more quality time on strategic thinking, market innovations, and operational breakthroughs, and there will be no need to have a special name or "campaign" around the process at all; it will simply be how your organization is run.

TIPS FOR AVOIDING THE SLUMPS

- Anticipate the predictable points where slumps occur during the Execution Phase and design specific plans into your transformation game plan to avoid them.
- After a successful Launch, make a clear shift into the *ballast-and-keel* role by continuing to communicate the same transformation messages and firmly holding the focus on the Transformation Initiatives.
- Rigorously assess progress on the corporate Transformation Initiatives and the process itself at a midcourse point during the first performance year and make any required course correction.

Notes

1. This chapter was adapted in part from Robert H. Miles and Michael Kanazawa, BIG Ideas to BIG Results: Leading Corporate Transformations in a Disruptive World, Second Edition. Pearson, 2016.
2. This expanded discussion of the pre-dictable "slumps and humps" during the Execute Phase of a corporate transformation and how to engage and overcome them, initially appeared in Robert H. Miles, "Accelerating Corporate Transformations – Don't Lose Your Nerve!" Harvard Business Review, January–February 2010.

CHAPTER 10

Transformation Leader
Reflections on the Role

The Moving Finger writes; and, having writ,
Moves on: nor all thy Piety nor Wit
Shall lure it back to cancel half a Line,
Nor all thy Tears wash out a Word of it.

— Rubaiyat of Omar Khayyam, The Astronomer-Poet of Persia, 1859

It is customary in the final chapter of a book to highlight the most important dimensions of the subject covered and summarize the major points. I have written three previous books on transformation leadership, which are built upon in this one. All were derived from my privileged access in the unique role as principal process architect of ACT-based transformations in a variety of private and public institutions. As a result, this book is intended to be a definitive guide for Transformation Leaders, consisting of both a comprehensive exploration of this complex subject and a granular treatment into how to articulate it. In this case, to understand the full complexity of rapid transformation and how to simplify and reliably lead or support it.

Given this purpose, I have chosen to focus on whether it has been achieved in the book by asking you, the reader, how prepared you now are to lead or support a rapid transformation? Hopefully, the Guide will have added to your store of knowledge beyond other, more incrementally focused but also important leadership skills, such as continuous improvement techniques and tactical change management methodologies.

To this end, I have prepared the following self-assessment of your comprehension of and preparation for leading or supporting a rapid transformation when such a career opportunity arises. It is comprehensive, but not exhaustive. Hopefully, the brief survey in Exhibit 10.1 will help you reflect on what you have learned and build your confidence in taking on this essential task in complex organizations, one that has heretofore been elusive to many.

DOI: 10.4324/9781003272724-10

EXHIBIT 10.1   Reader's Comprehensive Survey

Transformation Leadership:
A Guided Reflection

Please rate each question on a five-point scale: 5 = Yes, 3 = Maybe, 1 = No

- Do I know how to gauge the magnitude of the embedded "Inhibitors" to rapid transformation in my organization? ☐
- Can I identify the kinds of "Accelerators" that I will need to put in place to reliably implement rapid transformation? ☐
- Do I understand the role of Speed in transformation success? And the parts that simplicity of concept and compression of process have to do with productive speed in transformation? ☐
- Do I understand the concepts of "creating safe passage" and "structured dialogue" and how to seed them into our leadership function? ☐
- Am I able and ready to deal with unaligned leaders? ☐
- Am I convinced that a simple, but comprehensive transformation game plan is the best way to proceed? ☐
- Am I committed to stick to a roadmap with specific dates that reveals when and how everyone will be involved in the key transformation events through the first year and a half –and am I willing to announce it up front to everyone in the organization? ☐
- Do I get the importance of a rapid high-engagement cascade to engage, align and energize all our employees? ☐
- Am I willing to stick to a no-cut attendance rule in all transformation leadership events? ☐
- Do I understand what it means to "do more ON less" in shaping the Transformation Initiatives? ☐
- Will I be willing to commit to personally lead the transformation -- through all phases – until we achieve breakthrough performance? ☐
- Will I be able to create an environment in which our transformation is leader-led at all levels, with internal and external professionals in supporting roles? ☐
- Am I aware of the importance of quick starts and early successes in creating a basis for action? ☐
- Do I appreciate the need to align our values with the new performance and behavioral expectations? ☐
- Will I be able to create a clear line of sight from my Commitments to Action (CTAs) to those of the first line supervisors and employees? ☐
- Do I understand the side-benefits of leading with a rapid, leader-led, high-engagement transformation game plan? ☐
- Can I anticipate and minimize the predictable "humps and slumps" during the first performance year of execution? ☐
- Do I understand how to play a "ballast and keel" role during the execution phase? ☐
- Am I convinced of the need to kick off Year Two with a re-launch of a streamlined version of the transformation process to re-engage everyone and accelerate the progress? ☐

Bonus Question: What is the meaning of this ACT Formula: *Speed = Simplicity x Compression?* Identify a half dozen ways in which a Transformation Leader can increase simplicity and compression in the organization to accelerate transformation.

It has been said many times in this guide that a well-designed and orchestrated transformation has several important side benefits beyond the rapid achievement of its major initiatives and behavior-change goals. First, it must be designed with care up front to create "safe passage" for constructive dialogue and throughout the Launch, Cascade, and Execute phases for speed through simplicity in concepts and compression of processes. In the middle of the Launch Phase, it must be refined for crisp focus and top-to-bottom alignment, and down the stretch for leader-led employee engagement at all levels. Finally, your transformation must be respectful of the predictable humps and slumps during execution. If designed and implemented well, such a transformation overlay can gradually meld into and greatly strengthen the day-to-day management process, enrich leadership skills throughout the organization, and enhance its agility and culture.

Indeed, the streamlined approach to rapid transformation articulated in this book is probably the manner in which the contemporary organization should be led anyway.

Appendix 1

INITIAL EXECUTIVE INTERVIEWS: SENIOR AND EXTENDED LEADERSHIP TEAMS

Please review this interview protocol before meeting with Bob Miles to provide your answers to the questions.

PURPOSES

The purposes of this initial round of interviews with Bob Miles are:

- To obtain timely information from senior executives to guide planning of the launch of the next phase in the ongoing transformation of the company

- To give you an opportunity to get acquainted with Bob Miles, who will be assisting you and me in leading this effort.

METHODS

- Conduct confidential one-hour interview protocol with members of the Senior and Extended Leadership Teams.

- Interviewee identities will remain anonymous; recording will be verbatim.

Part I: Overall Assessment of Leadership Readiness

Ia. How would you describe the *overall magnitude of change* that will be required to successfully launch and realize the next phase in the transformation of the company?

Ib. What are the *three most important changes or improvements* that must take place in the company for it to be successful?

Ic. What are the *three most difficult obstacles* in the path of the company's transformation?

Id. What *kinds of help* do you and your senior colleagues need to successfully lead this effort?

Ie. If the transformation of the company is successful, what *characteristics* should the company exhibit by year end?

Part II: Preliminary Total Systems Diagnosis

What *major changes or improvements* need to be made in the following aspects of the organization (see definitions in the Appendix; Exhibit A.1) if the company is to become highly successful?

IIa. Strategies

IIb. Structure

IIc. Infrastructure

IId. People

IIe. Culture

IIf. Competencies

EXHIBIT A.1   Total-System Framework

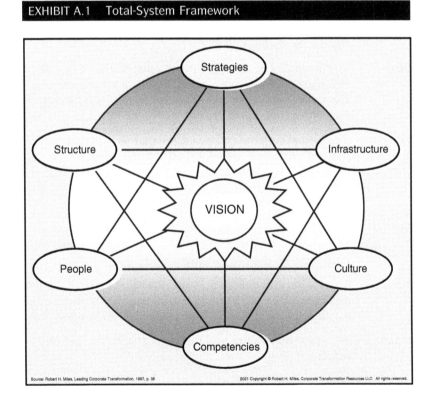

Source: Robert H. Miles, Leading Corporate Transformation, 1997, p. 36   2021 Copyright © Robert H. Miles, Corporate Transformation Resources LLC. All rights reserved.

Part III: Functioning of the Leadership Team

IIIa. How would you describe the *functioning* of the Leadership Team?

IIIb. What *specific changes* need to be made in order for the Leadership Team to be able to function in the most successful manner?

IIIc. What does the Leadership Team *need from the CEO* [or Transformation Leader] in order to be able to successfully lead this next phase in the transformation of the company?

IIId. What *immediate issues* does the Leadership Team need to resolve within the next 90 days?

GLOSSARY OF TERMS

Vision A succinct summary statement of the desired future state of the organization

Strategies The primary basis upon which an organization allocates resources to differentiate itself from competitors, creates customer value, and achieves exemplary performance in order to realize its vision

Structure The formal structural arrangements of the organization that delineate its basic units of authority and accountability, and the "overlays" that regulate the interdependencies that the formal arrangements create

Infrastructure The formal systems and processes that reinforce the intentions of the organization's structure and strategies including the basic measurement, control, planning, information, human resource, operations, communication, and resource allocation systems

People The nature of the workforce including work experience, skills, needs, preferences, maturity level, perceptions, orientations, and diversity, as well as the prevailing view of the role of the workforce in the organization

Culture The values and beliefs that are shared by most of the people in an organization and the style and behavior of its leaders; more a matter of what people and leaders do than what they say

Competencies The core competencies of the organization as a whole; what an organization does *particularly* well.

Appendix 2

EXTENDED LEADERSHIP TEAM MEETING 1: NOTEBOOK SKELETON

Driving a Successful Transformation Extended Leadership Team #1 (ELT1)

EXHIBIT A.2A   Meeting #1: Purposes

Purposes:

❏ To Refine the Business Realities, Strategic Vision and Business Success Model

❏ To understand the company's approach to transformation

❏ To Provide Feedback to the Co-Champions on the Preliminary Transformation Initiatives

❏ To Understand the Core Behavioral Expectations

❏ To Understand the Cascading Process to Engage All Managers and Employees

❏ To prepare Members of the ELT to Lead the company's Transformation

EXHIBIT A.2B   Compressed Agenda for ELT1 Meeting

Agenda:

0830	Welcome	
0845	Orientation to the Day	R. Miles
0900	"DrivingSuccessful Transformation:" An Introduction	

      • Presentation (45 min)
         ✓ Our current Business Realities
         ✓ Our Strategic Vision
         ✓ Our Business Model
         ✓ Leadership Readiness

0945	Accelerated Corporate Transformation Process: An Overview (45 min)	R. Miles

      ▪ Framework for Leaders
      ▪ Process Architecture
      ▪ Roadmap

1030	Break	
1045	Introduction to the major Transformation Initiatives and Co-Champions	
1100	_____ Initiative	Co-Champions:

      • Presentation (30 min)
      • Tablework (40 min)
      • Sample Reports (20 min)

1230	Lunch	
1315	_____ Initiative	Co-Champions:

      • Presentation (30 min)
      • Tablework (40 min)
      • Sample Reports (20 min)

1445	Break	
1500	_____ Initiative	Co-Champions:

      • Presentation (30 min)
      • Tablework (40 min)
      • Sample Reports (20 min)

1630	Coffee Break	
1645	Values & Leadership Behaviors	

      • Presentation (10 min)
      • Tablework (30 min)
      • Sample Reports (10 min)

1735	Cascade Orientation and Vedio	B. Miles
1800	Call to Action and Next Steps	
1830	Adjourn	

EXHIBIT A.2C   ELT 1 Notebook Tabs

Tabs:

1. Welcome

2. Orientation to the Day

3. "Driving Successful Transformation:" An Introduction

4. Accelerated Corporate Transformation Process: An Overview

5. Introduction to the Major Transformation Initiatives and Co-Champions

6. _____ Initiative

7. _____ Initiative

8. _____ Initiative

9. Values & Leadership Behaviors

10. Cascade Orientation and Video

11. Call to Action and Next Steps

Appendix 3

MID-COURSE ASSESSMENT OF TRANSFORMATION PROGRESS: FEEDBACK FROM SENIOR AND EXTENDED LEADERSHIP TEAM MEMBERS

PURPOSES

- To obtain mid-course feedback from members of the Senior Leadership Team and Extended Leadership Team about the overall progress made with the transformation effort

- To obtain specific recommendations for improvement regarding important aspects of the process

- To learn how to re-invigorate the transformation process and integrate it into the management system.

METHODS

- Conduct confidential, 1¼-hour structured interviews (see attached protocol) with the SLT and ELT executives.

- Interviewee identities will remain anonymous; recording will be verbatim.

- Interviews to be conducted within the following two weeks (dates) and delivered initially at the next SLT1 Meeting.

INTERVIEW PROTOCOL

A. Primary Questions

1. What is your *overall assessment* of the progress made so far with the transformation of the company?

2. What has been working *particularly well*? Please explain.

3. What has *not* worked well? Why? (Please be as specific as possible.)

4. Has the transformation process *changed any of the ways* you run your part of the company?

□Yes □No

If Yes, how?

If No, why not?

B. Specific Aspects

5. Are there any Areas of Focus in your part of the company that did *not* get the support you needed to be able to achieve significant improvement? □Yes□No

If Yes, please identify the specific areas and what support would be helpful.

6. In your view, what are the best opportunities (those that will add the greatest value) for the *integration* of the transformation and the way we run the business? Please be specific and explain why you think so.

7. Have the *Quarterly "Challenges"* that are announced at the ELT meetings been useful in helping you advance progress on the Initiatives in your part of the company? □Yes□No

Explain:

8. Have the *CEO's Challenges* been useful in helping you advance progress in your part of the company? □Yes□No

Explain:

9. Have the *Best Practice* recommendations from the quarterly ELT Meetings been useful in helping you advance progress in your part of the company? □Yes□No

Explain:

10a. What is your assessment of the role played by the *Senior Leadership Team*?

10b. What should *the Senior Leadership Team do differently* in the future to be more effective in supporting your efforts to drive the transformation effort? Please be specific.

11. What specific improvements are needed to make the *Cascade process* work more effectively?

a. at the **Supervisor** level?

b. at the **Employee** level?

12. What specific recommendations would you make to improve the effectiveness of the ELT meetings?

13. Please assess the **progress of each Initiative** (on a scale of **1** = very little progress to **10** = very great progress):

    a. _____*Initiative* (Rating: _____) Please explain.

    b. _____*Initiative* (Rating: _____) Please explain.

    c. _____*Initiative* (Rating: _____) Please explain.

14. Stepping back from everything that has been covered in this interview, what are the *three* most important things the Senior Leadership Team needs to do *to reinvigorate the transformation process and successfully integrate it into the way we run the enterprise?*

    a.

    b.

    c.

15. How do you feel about the *role you personally have played* in the transformation effort? Please explain.

INDEX

Page numbers in italics indicate a figures.

For Product Safety Concerns and Information please contact our EU
representative GPSR@taylorandfrancis.com
Taylor & Francis Verlag GmbH, Kaufingerstraße 24, 80331 München, Germany

www.ingramcontent.com/pod-product-compliance
Ingram Content Group UK Ltd.
Pitfield, Milton Keynes, MK11 3LW, UK
UKHW050932180425
457613UK00015B/372